Scottish Borders Library Service

3 4144 0079 7008 7

N-FICTION   994 ✕

# AUSTRALIA
# A HISTORY

# AUSTRALIA
# A HISTORY

## MIKE WALKER

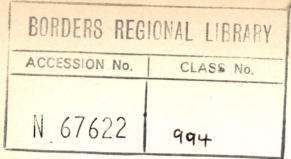

BORDERS REGIONAL LIBRARY

| ACCESSION No. | CLASS No. |
|---|---|
| N 67622 | 994 |

An OPTIMA book

© Mike Walker 1987

First published in 1987 by
Macdonald Optima, a division of
Macdonald & Co. (Publishers) Ltd

A BPCC PLC company

*All rights reserved*

No part of this publication may be reproduced,
stored in a retrieval system, or transmitted,
in any form or by any means without the prior
permission in writing of the publisher, nor be
otherwise circulated in any form of binding or
cover other than that in which it is published
and without a similar condition including this
condition being imposed on the subsequent
purchaser.

British Library Cataloguing in Publication Data
Walker, Mike
    Australia: a history.
    1. Australia—History
    I. Title
    994      DU110

    ISBN 0-356-14570-0

Macdonald & Co. (Publishers) Ltd
3rd Floor
Greater London House
Hampstead Road
London NW1 7QX

Photoset in 11pt Century by
🅰 Tek Art Ltd, Croydon, Surrey

Printed and bound in Great Britain by
The Guernsey Press Co. Ltd,
Guernsey, Channel Islands

# CONTENTS

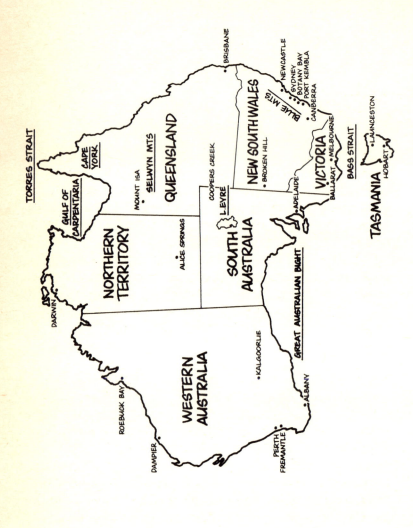

# PREFACE

Australia is like nowhere else on earth. Its landscape includes thousands of miles of empty desert and tropical rain forests, its mammals are throwbacks to an earlier stage of evolution, and the variety and voracity of its flies is equalled only by the appetite of its spiders.

The French scientist Cuvier compared it to a fragment of another star, dropped from the sky to rest on our world, but for many thousands of years the first Australians adapted themselves to this environment, creating a rich and complex way of life until . . . until . . .

What happened then is the story the BBC Radio 4 series *Australia* (and this book based on it) sets out to tell. What happened to the Aborigines? What happened to the convicts dragged halfway round the world to live or die by their own efforts? What happened to the greedy and violent men who sought profit? What happened to the idealists, the explorers, the men and women who settled and worked the land, the city slum dwellers, the bushrangers, the labour leaders, the businessmen and artists and others whose lives have gone to make up Australia?

Mark Twain, after his travels in the country, said that its history 'is full of surprises and adventures, and incongruities, and contradictions, and incredibilities, but they are all true, they all happened'. Many of those surprises and incongruities were recorded by the pioneers and are as fresh now as when they were set down in the lee of a wagon during a sheep drive or in the cramped and soaking cabin of an immigrant ship. So this is not an academic history of facts and treaties, though all the important moments are there. It is the story of the people, often in their own words for, as Ian Mudie says in his poem *They'll Tell You About Me:*

> '. . . yesterday I was rumour,
> today I am legend,
> tomorrow, history.
> If you'd like to know more of me
> inquire at the pub at Tennant Creek,
> or at any drovers' camp,
> or shearing-shed,
> or shout any bloke in any bar a drink;
> they'll tell you about me,
> they'll tell you more than I know myself.
> After all, they were the ones that created me,
> even though I'm bigger than any of them now.
> – in fact, I'm all of them rolled into one.'

This book of *Australia* reflects the radio series and both are indebted to many people. Foremost is Shaun Macloughlin, series producer/director and friend, whose energy, commitment and creativity made the venture possible. Andrew Lawrence brought skill and sensitivity to the technical aspects of the series, as did Elizabeth Parker, whose music illuminated many dark corners. Iain Hunter and Helen Thomas gave far beyond the call of duty, as did Rosamund Landor, Tessa Lecomber, Rebecca Curtis, Frances Byrne, Jenny Littlewood and Alex, who phoned for taxis, Jane Macloughlin, who gave time, friendship and food, and Bill Leimbach who started it all. The series and the book were fortunate to have the help of some of Australia's leading historians. I should like to thank

Professors Geoffrey Blainey, Manning Clark, Humphrey McQueen, Eric Wilmot, Dame Professor Leoni Kramer, Dr Ross Fitzgerald and Edmund Campion.

For the Aboriginal chapter, *The Dreamer Wakes*, I am grateful to Michelle Rowlands for her knowledge and enthusiasm in the recording of many interviews. I would also like to thank Charles Perkins, Eve Fesle Snr, Eve Fesle Jnr, Kath Walker, Pat Dodson, Robert Brofoe, Shortie O'Neill, Marcia Langton and Yami Lester. For the later chapters, I am indebted to Barry Jones, Chris Maroukis, Dorothy Green, David Malouf and Clem Semmler.

For permission to use copyright material, I would like to thank: Professor R.M. Berndt for his translation of a fragment from the *Dulnguly Cycle* of the Mudbara tribe; the Hakluyt Society for extracts from Captain Cook's journals; the Alexander Turnball library for extracts from Ensign Best's journal; A.P. Watt Ltd and Peta Paine Pty Ltd for extracts from *We of the Never-Never*; Jennifer Isaacs for a story and poem from *Australian Dreaming*; Renée Mudie for part of Ian Mudie's poem, *They'll Tell You About Me*. Every effort has been made to trace copyright holders, but if any have not been acknowledged, the publisher would be pleased to be informed.

Finally, thanks to Anthony Goff and Liz Cree, my editor Cécile Landau and, most of all, to my wife Jennifer for her faith, support and advice.

# 1.
# IN THE DREAMING

The day breaks – the first rays of
the rising sun, stretching her arms.
Daylight breaking as the sun rises to
    her feet.
Sun rising, scattering the darkness,
    lighting up the land.

When the British laid claim to Australia in the
eighteenth century, they were the last, though perhaps
the most acquisitive, in a long line of visitors and
immigrants. As they stepped ashore with flags flying,
bayonets fixed and eyes peeled, they found abundant
evidence of prior possession, but it did not occur to
them that the Australians, the first Australians, might
have or want a right to own the land they had lived in
for over 40,000 years.

## Aborigines

Where these firstcomers originated is a mystery. They
might have come from different places at different
times. What we do know is the route some of them took
– down through the islands of Indonesia. During the
ice ages the sea level was lower and the islands were
closer together – but the last jump into the unknown
could well have lead them off the edge of the world.
    Whether it was the adventurous or the unlucky who
went first, the process of migration started and

continued over thousands of years, though we cannot
be sure if it went in waves or in a regular flow. There
are still many questions to be answered, but whenever
that first crossing was made, the new arrivals found a
very different landscape confronting them. They might
have noticed, uneasily, that there was no bamboo to
repair their rafts for a return trip. During their
journey they had crossed a line (later named after the
naturalist Wallace) which divides the flora and fauna
of Asia from that of Australasia. The plants were
adapted to a totally different environment and had to
be approached with care. The insects and reptiles were
much as they might be elsewhere in the world but the
mammals they encountered were the earliest examples
of life's evolutionary advance from reptiles.


## Animal life
These living fossils, like the echidna and platypus,
were so strange that the first scientists to examine
them during the nineteenth century thought they were
the victims of trickery and refused to believe that the
platypus laid eggs. It was not until one was shot with
an egg inside her that the experts faced the impossible
– an egg-laying mammal which suckled its newly-
hatched young not from a nipple but with milk fat
exuding like sweat through the skin.

The Aborigines, after a first curious glance, perhaps
took the practical course and ate the beasts. They were
hunters and the country must have seemed to their
delighted gaze like a larder full of peaceful marsupial
inhabitants used to a life virtually without predators.
Some of these marsupials, recalled in Aboriginal
stories, were massive indeed. Diprotodon, a grass eater,
weighed in at two tons and resembled our rhinoceros;
genyornis was the height of an emu but four times
heavier; there was a giant kangaroo, able to browse on
leaves three metres above the ground; a wombat over a
metre high; a marsupial lion which might or might not

11

have been carnivorous; and the thylacine, the Tasmanian tiger.

They were all to disappear, vanquished by their size and temperament, the climate or even the dingo, a placental mammal of great appetite which arrived with a later wave of immigrants. The smaller marsupials managed things better and thrived. So did the flies, which evolved more than 2,000 species to plague man and animals, and the spiders, which developed a 1,000 species to plague the flies.

## Survival

The newcomers were nomads who moved in small groups, each adopting enough land to provide food over the turn of the seasons. They were young people in an old land, where they might cross stony deserts to reach lush mango swamps, snowy mountains or grassy plains. They adapted, learning to hunt in new ways. Using a remarkable talent for mimicry, they called the crabs from their holes in the swamps with clicks of the tongue or could freeze fleeing goanna with the cry of a hawk. A boomerang could knock a fruit-bat from the sky, a spear thrower hit a distant, moving target with pinpoint accuracy. Their tools, though basic and few, performed the tasks required of them. They fished in the swamps, rivers and the sea with basket traps, lines, nets and bone hooks. In some places they used magic, cutting off the top joint of a child's finger and casting it into the water for the fish. When the owner of the finger called, the fish felt compelled to answer and swim into the net. They used fire too, carrying a glowing stick wherever they went. They used fire for warmth, to drive prey from cover, to make smoke signals or to banish insects, and sometimes for fun burning millions of acres of scrubland for the sheer joy of it.

They learnt to survive in hard times and in unlikely places, finding, for instance that during drought some toads buried themselves, bloated with water, under dry

river beds; if you stamped on the mud the toads
thought it was raining and croaked, providing a handy
squeeze pack for a thirsty traveller.

**The Dreaming**
Physically they were of many types, and their
languages and dialects were numbered in the
thousands. The tools they used and traded, how and
where they hunted, the pictures and stories they made
all changed as they spread around the country. But in
one thing they were the same and it was that which
gave their life meaning.

The Dreaming is almost impossible to explain and, at
the very least, confusing to demonstrate. It is a world
view which holds everything in the life of an Aborigine
– the mythic past of the great ancestors; the physical
present; the animals and their intimate partnership
with man; the law, as it was given and is now
practised. In one sense it is the interaction of time and
eternity and in another it is kicking a stone and
watching the pattern it makes as it rolls away down a
hillside. The actions and intentions of the ancestors
live in the present in an entirely concrete way. Yet the
Aborigines do not go to church or temple. Each is a
living prayer – every breath, every song, every footstep
is a part of their Dreaming and their religious belief.

The Dreaming informed their lives, their laws and
their customs, and they lived within it, reflecting the
years in story and song. They tell of the passing of the
great kangaroos, of journeys magic and real or both,
because they could navigate by the Dreamtime stories
as well as we can with a map. They even record the
ending of the last ice age when the waters rose and the
country lost one-seventh of its area.

Disputes within groups were sometimes settled by
bloody battles, but more often by ritual or by men who
were learned in law and tradition. They were not a
cruel people, though their lives, dictated by the
seasons, could be hard. If there was famine, they all

suffered; when there was enough, it was enough for all.
Infants or the old might be left to perish in times of
hardship, but this was the price of survival for a
nomadic people. Too many or too few and the balance
was upset. Get it right and they could live as well as or
better than the majority of the world's population had
through a long and troubled history.

As Geoffrey Blainey has pointed out, eighteenth-
century Aborigines would have felt that a German
peasant's hut was a scene of poverty and want. They
had leisure, music, art, stories and dance, laws and
customs, the freedom to be what they wished –
powerful or rich in influence, to know the mysteries, to
be a good hunter, to find a strong husband or a good
wife. It was a life as rich and harsh as nature itself,
but elsewhere in the world men were beginning to
dream a different dream of what there might be
through the Pillars of Hercules.

## EARLY VOYAGES

The Greeks, passionate to know why and how,
reasoned that if the earth were round the laws of
physics required something on the other side to balance
the weight of Europe and Asia; otherwise, surely, the
earth would tip over.

Theopompus talked of a 'land which in greatness is
infinite and has green meadows and pasture plot and
big and mighty beasts'. Later St Augustine wondered if
it were possible to imagine anything more absurd than
inhabitants in the opposite regions of the earth. In the
thirteenth century Friar Roger Bacon said some
considered that paradise might be in the antipodes.

Not until the fifteenth century and the beginnings of
the Portuguese Empire did Europeans make any moves
towards the *terra australis incognita*, the unknown
southern land. Using the infant and often inaccurate
science of navigation, Portuguese sailors crept down
the coast of Africa, keeping land in sight to their left,

fearful of being boiled alive around the next cape. The exploration was a mixture of Henry the Navigator's idealism and investors' hopes of huge profits. Within a hundred years, the Portuguese had shown the way to Indonesia and opened up the East Indies.

There is no record of their landing in Australia. That honour (if the Chinese didn't get there during the fifteenth century) belongs to a Dutchman, Wilhelm Jansz. In 1606 he sailed down through the Malay Archipelago and touched on the north coast in the region of the Arnhemland. Under the impression it was New Guinea, he mapped part of the coast, and sailed back home. Later in the same year a Spaniard, Louis Torres, passed through the straits which now bear his name between Cape York and Papua New Guinea, but it was the Dutch who were really interested in the area. They saw an opportunity for high profit where the Dutch East India Company with its ships could take and hold a commercial empire.

In 1616 Captain Dirk Hartog landed on the west coast, and left behind a pewter plate inscribed with his name. The Company then included in sailing orders specific instructions for its captains 'to land at different places to examine the country and . . . pay particular attention to any gold, silver, lead, copper or precious stones there may be'.

## Van Diemen and Tasman

In 1636 a new governor of Batavia was announced, Anthony van Diemen, an intelligent, well-read man who had informed himself on the Spanish and Portuguese voyages in the area. He hoped to extend Dutch possessions and influence in the east, and was shrewd enough to stress the chance of huge profits to his company backers. They eventually financed an expedition under the command of Abel Tasman, a hardbitten and experienced sailor. But there was no gold or silver on the island Tasman sighted on 24th November 1642. He 'bestowed upon it the name

Anthony van Diemen's land, in honour of our great governor', and raised a flag. There were no inhabitants to be seen, 'though we thought that some were not far away and watching us'.

On his return to Batavia, Tasman found unhappy investors. Where were the gold, the silver, the new trade routes? Van Diemen, with his eye on long-term rewards, persuaded them to pay for another voyage to map the north coast of what was called New Holland and was at least being thought of as separate from *terra australis*, which was assumed to lie farther south.

By the end of his second voyage, Tasman had provided an outline of most of the north coast, an astounding achievement which received a predictable response from the money men: 'We cannot anticipate any great results from the continuation of such discoveries, which entail further expenditure from the Company'.

Van Diemen died in 1645. Tasman got neither thanks nor reward, and Dutch exploration of New Holland virtually ceased.

### Dampier and the Aborigines

The next visitor was an Englishman, also interested in gold but with an understanding of the sea and sailing which amounted to genius. William Dampier was a farmer's son who went to sea in 1670 at the comparatively late age of 18. After a while spent drifting, he ended up in Jamaica where he joined the buccaneers, more, he said, to indulge his curiosity than to get rich. He took part in the sack of Portobello and joined a number of cruises, on one of which, as second-in-command, he was nearly eaten by the starving crew.

Dampier's first contact with New Holland came when a privateering expedition in the Pacific went wrong and his ship, crippled by a series of storms, made landfall on the north-west coast. After a series of adventures, including shipwreck and escape from the Dutch, Dampier arrived back in Britain and published an account of his voyage. On the strength of this, he was asked by the government to take the ship *Roebuck* back to the south seas.

On 31st August 1699 he stepped ashore on the west coast near what is now known as Roebuck Bay. The landing party were armed with cutlasses and rifles and carried pickaxes and shovels to dig wells. They were not unobserved. Dampier wrote:

> 'While we were at work there came nine or ten of the natives to a small hill and stood there threatening us . . . I took two men with me and went purposely to catch one of them, of whom I might learn where they got their fresh water. But they being four or five times our number thought to seize us, so a nimble young man that was with me ran towards them, and they, for some time ran away before him. But he overtaking them, they faced about and fought him. He had a cutlass and they had wooden lances, with which they were too hard for him. I discharged my gun to scare them but though it a little frightened them, they soon learnt to despise it, tossing up their hands and crying "Pooh, pooh, pooh".'

He was able to map the coastline, but the poor condition of the *Roebuck* forced him to turn for home after only five weeks. The condition of the ship was even worse than Dampier suspected, and it sank off Ascension Island where most of the supplies and valuable documents were lost. After a couple of months living on yams and turtles, the mariners were rescued.

Back in London, where he faced a court-martial for losing the *Roebuck* (rather unfair, since the ship was falling apart when they gave it to him), Dampier wrote a bestseller on his trip in which, among scientific observations, he gives his opinion of the natives: 'They all of them have the most unpleasant looks and the worst features of any people that ever I saw, though I have seen a great variety of savages.'

What the Aborigines made of William Dampier is not recorded, though at about this time they were making peaceful contacts along the north coast with Indonesian fishermen from Macassa. Trade soon began, with young Aborigines helping aboard the ships, perhaps even travelling back across the seas. Long-stemmed pipes, tamarind trees and the Van Dyke beard were all introduced and can still be seen on the north coast. The contact was beneficial to both sides but the time was not far distant when more acquisitive eyes would be cast on Australian shores.

## Cook lands

On 19 April 1770 a young scientist stood on a cramped ship's deck bracing himself against a heavy swell. He was to write of that day in his journal: 'With the first day light this morn the land was seen. It rose in gentle sloping hills which had the appearance of the highest fertility . . . At noon a smoke was seen a little way inland.'

Beside the young man, whose name was Joseph Banks, stood the captain of the ship, a middle-aged Yorkshireman, James Cook. His notes were technical, as befitted his position and responsibilities: 'At 5 set the topsail close reef'd and at 6 saw land extending from NE to west at the distance of 5 or 6 leagues, having 80 fathom water, a fine sandy bottom.'

The ship was the *Endeavour*. Its mission was two-fold: to observe the transit of Venus from the island of Tahiti and, secretly, to search for that old hope, the counterweight continent, *terra australis*. The astronomical readings had been taken, but the continent remained obstinately *incognita*, and after a year and a half at sea the *Endeavour* was heading home. Cook's instructions made no mention of New Holland, but he decided to follow its east coast and make for Batavia, where his ship could be laid up and repaired before the long haul back to Britain. It was a hazardous undertaking for there were no maps or charts, but Cook and Banks, in the scientific spirit of the times, could not resist the opportunity to inspect an unknown coastline.

They landed and named Botany Bay where they were shouted at by spear-waving Aborigines, 'but to little purpose', as Cook wrote, 'for neither of us could understand one word they said'. They threw some nails and beads ashore and departed. More than four months and many landfalls later, after a voyage during which they nearly sank on the Barrier Reef, Cook applied to New Holland the instructions he'd been given about *terra australis*: 'You are to, with the consent of the natives, take possession of convenient situations in the name of the King of Great Britain.'

On a small, conveniently uninhabited island off Cape York, Cook set up a flag pole, hoisted English colours and 'took possession of the whole eastern coast by the name of New South Wales'. Three volleys of small arms were fired and answered with three broadsides from the *Endeavour's* cannons.

The Spanish had found the land and left it to its Dreaming. The Dutch had come, named it and departed for richer pickings. The Indonesians had visited every summer and gone away every autumn. But now the British had found it and would not let it go. Time had come to the timeless land and nothing would be the same again.

# 2.
# THE MOST VALUABLE ACQUISITION

In 1776 Britain's North American colonies declared themselves independent. The British army was beaten and the country shocked. It was also faced with a serious problem. For over 60 years the authorities had been sending convicts to America where they were sold as indentured workers, a convenient and profitable enterprise with tradesmen fetching £15 and women up to £10. The revolution stopped this, but convicts kept on coming from British courts.

During the 1770s and 80s there were 160 offences which carried the death penalty, from treason and murder to stealing linen from the bleaching grounds and cutting down trees in an avenue. It wasn't surprising if juries often failed to convict or chose lesser charges which resulted in imprisonment. Unfortunately, there was nowhere to send the convicts except the prisons and hulks and these became more and more overcrowded. Something had to be done.

A solution came in a proposal by J M Mattra, who had sailed with Cook as a midshipman. His family were American loyalists dispossessed by the Revolution and he suggested that those who had remained loyal to the Crown should be compensated with land in New South Wales. They could provide a base from which the British navy might 'powerfully annoy' either the Dutch or Portuguese in the event of war. The proposal was not welcome until Mattra added the possibility of using the country as a prison. No one was likely to escape, he said, and the convicts would have no choice but to work or starve.

The resettlement scheme never had a chance but an answer to the convict problem and a naval base in the Pacific were appealing. In addition, the native flax could be spun for canvas and cord, the tall Norfolk Island pines would provide replacement masts, and all the work would be done by unpaid labour.

On 17 January 1786 Lord Sydney, Secretary of State at the Home Office, informed the Commissioners of the Treasury that the King had commanded them 'to take immediate measure to send out of the kingdom such convicts as are under order of transportation'. They were to gather a fleet large enough to carry 778 convicts and such 'provisions, necessaries and implements' as would be needed for their survival.

## Arthur Phillip

It was quite an order. There were 40 cross-cut saws at 10 shillings each; hand saws at 5 shillings; 300 chisels, 7 pence each; there were wheelbarrows, pickaxes and ploughs; 600,000 nails of various lengths; 1,000 squares of glass; for each male convict for a year, two jackets, four pairs of woollen drawers, one hat, three shirts, four pairs of worsted stockings, three smocks, three trousers and three pairs of shoes, in all costing £3. The list went on and on, amounting to £3,286, not counting the food supplies for the convicts and the marines who would guard them. A complex business and, as most of it was done throught private tender, it was not surprising that a few pockets were better lined as a result. Certainly the man in charge was to be bedevilled by shortages and dishonesty and was to make himself thoroughly unpopular as a result of his protests.

His name was Arthur Phillip. He was a captain in the Royal Navy, 48 years old, a slight sallow-skinned man with his right upper front tooth missing. He had been on half-pay, without a ship, for the last five years, occupying his time as a farmer near Cheltenham. He got the job through the influence of a neighbour, George Rose, who was Undersecretary at the Treasury, not that there were a lot of candidates. The navy didn't like handling convicts and the prospects of promotion in New South Wales, like the prospects of success, were low.

Phillip seemed to be a run-of-the-mill officer, competent and unexciting, but he was a man with a vision which enabled him to see the proposed colony as something more than a dumping-ground for convicts. He looked forward to a free society with a base of hard-working settlers. It was an enlightened and reasonable idea, reflecting the best hopes of the eighteenth century, but Phillip was more than a simple dreamer, he had a core of persistence and common sense which at times triumphed over even the civil service.

The navy had provided two vessels, the *Sirius* as flagship and a sloop, *Supply*. Six transports and three cargo ships were hired from private contractors. The fleet was gathered in the Port of London and loading began. When Phillip arrived to take command, he found many of the transports already full. Some convicts had been waiting on board for months, their quarters getting filthier by the day. He immediately had the ships cleared and cleaned out.

When the female convicts were loaded aboard the *Lady Penrhyn*, they were almost naked, filthy and ridden with fever. Some had babies or young children in so bad a state that Phillip clothed them with whatever was at hand. He complained, but the women were still waiting for their official clothing when the fleet sailed. It also went without documentation on the convicts or their sentences, without the Provost Marshal and without any ammunition for the marines' muskets. They did, however, have 200 copies of *Exercizes Against Lying*, 50 Woodward's *Caution to Swearers*, and 100 *Exhortations to Chastity*. These were

in the hands of the chaplain, Richard Johnson, pay
£182 per annum, and his wife Mary.

Phillip was not, as far as we know, a believer. He
saw religion as a force for order and even in his private
notes, where he laid out his hopes for the colony, the
accent is always on enthusiasm tempered by reason:

> 'Rewards and punishments must be left to the
> Governor. Death, I should think, will never be
> necessary. In fact I doubt if the fear of death ever
> prevented a man of no principle from committing a
> bad action. There is however one law I wish to
> take place from the moment we land: there can be
> no slavery in a free land and consequently no
> slaves.'

Loading was as complete as it was going to be by the
spring of 1787 and the fleet sailed to Portsmouth,
where many of the officers joined. Second-in-command
of the *Sirius*, with a dormant commission as governor
in case Phillip died, was Captain John Hunter, a
dependable and loyal sailor.

Among the junior officers was Lt Philip Gidley King,
an old friend who had served with Phillip and was
marked out to take charge of the settlement at Norfolk
Island, to be occupied at the same time as the
mainland. The best of the marines were Captain
Watkin Tench, a witty and observant young man;
Captain David Collins, the Judge Advocate of the
colony; and the doctor, John White, one of the few,
apart from Phillip, who had tried to improve the
conditions of the convicts.

These and a few others had open minds about the
enterprise. The rest saw it as the chance to turn a
quick profit and do as little work as possible. They
were supported in this by the marine commander and
Deputy Governor, Major Robert Ross, who appears to
have been a vain, short-tempered martinet, who
regarded every slight as a deadly insult.

The convicts were an unknown quantity. How they would adapt to the new land was a question at the bottom of everyone's list. They had come from all corners of the British Isles. Thomas Barratt had been sentenced to death in London for stealing a watch and some shirts. Perhaps because of his age – he was still in his teens – his sentence had been commuted to 14 years' transportation. James Ruse from Cornwall was a burglar; Ann Smith had stolen a pewter pot and, since this was by no means her first offence, got seven years; William Bryant, a fisherman from the West Country, was to have been hanged for forgery but ended up below decks, chained and confined by reinforced bulkheads through which holes had been cut for the guards' muskets to fire at any threat of trouble.

Labourers and domestic servants made up the majority. Phillip had asked for convicts with skills. He needed carpenters, farmworkers, blacksmiths, masons; what he got was the sweepings of the gaols, the troublemakers, the sick and the feeble-minded. He would have to make the best of the material at his disposal; anyone who could do a job would be given it, regardless of their past record.

On the evening before the fleet sailed an entertainment called 'Botany Bay' was put on in London. It was a frothy piece unconcerned with the harsh realities of the expedition, but then nobody cared much. The ships sailed to a deafening silence; there was no waving and hardly a mention in the newspapers as they headed out into the Atlantic.

## Transportation

Most of the convicts, fed up with months of waiting in port, were glad to be moving anywhere, though their notions of the country they were heading for were vague. The natives were waiting to eat the first man to step ashore, it was somewhere near China and there was gold in abundance.

There were births, deaths and accidents as the fleet

ploughed on. Ishmael Coleman, 'worn out by lowness of spirits and long and close confinement, resigned his breath without a pang'. A marine corporal shot himself in the foot. The officers visited among the ships when conditions allowed.

The ships called at Tenerife and Rio de Janeiro where they stocked up with plants they hoped would grow in New South Wales, including coffee, indigo and cotton. By November they had reached the Cape of Good Hope and Phillip transferred to the *Supply*, a faster ship than the *Sirius*. With three transports, he left the main fleet, intending to reach Botany Bay and establish a base camp before the rest arrived.

On the last day of December 1787 the advance squadron covered 180 miles. On 4th January they bettered that and, under low clouds, sighted the coast of Van Diemen's Land. The officers drank a toast and anchored for the night for fear of rocks. So far the wind had been kind. Now luck deserted them and they crawled along the eastern coast, not arriving at Botany Bay until 18th January. They observed occasional smoke and, at night, the twinkling of fires inland. As they rounded Point Solander and entered the bay they saw a small group of natives running along the shore waving their spears.

The ships dropped anchor on the north side of the bay at noon. Two days later the rest of the fleet hauled in and paid out their anchor cables. Dr White thought that the general good health was a sight 'at which every heart must rejoice'. David Collins agreed, particularly in view of the state in which the convicts had embarked. Only 36 people had died since leaving England – a stupendous achievement due in great part to Phillip's insistence on exercise and the constant cleaning of the convicts quarters. Though many had found the regime irksome, they owed it their lives.

**Sydney founded**
The overall feeling was of relief mixed with

apprehension. It was a delightfully warm day with a slight haze and a fair wind. The bay was presenting its best face. Watkin Tench felt like Ulysses returning to Ithaca.

Unfortunately, Phillip had already decided the place was totally unsuitable for a colony. The shore was swampy, there was not enough fresh water, the ships were buffeted by an east wind and the gently-shelving bottom of the bay made ship-to-shore unloading impossible. If Botany Bay was the best of New South Wales, they might as well turn around and go back home.

Sweeping aside his disappointment, Phillip took a small party in an open cutter and set off along the coast. He pinned his hopes on Port Jackson, a bay Captain Cook had named but not explored. To his considerable relief he found there 'the finest harbour in the world, in which a thousand sail of the line may ride in the most perfect security'. He returned with the good news to Botany Bay and the fleet prepared to move on for a last leg. But consternation was caused by two strange sails on the horizon, glimpsed and then lost. A day later they reappeared – two French ships, a scientific expedition under the navigator La Pérouse. The British extended a cautious welcome and sailed off to Port Jackson, from whence some convicts paid unofficial visits to the French. M. La Pérouse was scrupulous in returning them to the British.

Phillip had chosen a quiet cove for the first landing 'which I honoured with the name of Sydney'. The ground was thick with trees, and the first task was to clear a space near a fresh-water stream where a pole was erected, the flag run up and possession taken formally in the name of King George III. Toasts were drunk by Phillip and his officers, the marines shattered the silence with several vollies and, since it was evening, the flag was run down again. Only a few well-behaved convicts were ashore and Lt Clark, a young marine, found that first sunset peaceful with the tents

looking pretty among the trees and the camp fires
twinkling. It was 26th January 1788.

## The convicts ashore

The next morning the male convicts were unloaded. As
they came ashore they were handed axes, saws or bars
and told to start clearing the land. It was no easy task.
The axes and saws, of poor quality to begin with, were
soon blunted on the hard gum wood and, when the
trees were at last felled, such was their size that
moving them was almost impossible. There was a good
deal of frustration and confusion too as the supplies
were hurried ashore and dumped wherever there was
room.

Food for 500 labouring men, with mobile kitchens,
huge kettles of soup and fires to heat them must have
put a considerable strain on resources and space. Then
there were the blacksmiths' and carpenters' shops, the
setting up of tents for the marines and shelters for the
convicts, the animals, a piano someone had brought
and a canvas house Phillip had ordered in London.

The women came ashore on 1st February while the
worst storm the colonists had experienced was brewing.
As the thunder crashed and rain turned the ground to
liquid mud, the camp degenerated into anarchy. The
sailors from the transports, with bribes of rum, and the
marines, with promises of privilege, were making
assignations with the unattached women. The male
convicts, regarding the women as their natural allies,
responded with violence. The night passed riotously, an
explosion of relief after the confinement and anxiety of
the voyage. Phillip, knowing he could do nothing to
stop it, let it happen.

The next morning, as the sun dried the wet ground,
the bedraggled and hungover convicts were called
together and counted. Nine were missing, including
Ann Smith, who'd stolen the pewter pot. Throughout
the voyage she'd voiced her intention of running away
as soon as she got ashore, perhaps to that mythical

China over the hill or to the French who were still at Botany Bay.

After the count, Judge Advocate Collins read Phillip's commission, giving him command over a territory extending from Cape York in the north to the southern extremity of New South Wales, including all the adjacent islands in the Pacific Ocean. Phillip then spoke to the assembled convicts 'informing them of his intentions which were inevitably to cherish and render happy those who showed a disposition to amendment'. As for the rest, Tench went on to report, he would let 'the rigour of the law take its course against such as might dare to transgress the bounds prescribed'.

## Food problems

Food was going to be vital. Phillip knew that farming was going to be a struggle. The colony would be living off its supplies for some time to come. Theft of food would endanger everyone and he made it clear that it would be regarded as the most serious of crimes.

Within a month of the first landing, Phillip sent Lt King and a party of convicts to settle Norfolk Island, but this was a sideline and the struggle began to get established at Sydney. Results were not encouraging. After six months Dr White still had over 70 scurvy patients. Only four officers had huts, though this wasn't surprising with only four carpenters in the colony. The convicts were using old sails or had built makeshift shelters out of brushwood and rushes which burned down so often that fires were forbidden inside them. Solid building was hampered by lack of lime for cement. A house for Major Ross, of stone keyed with clay, literally melted away in the rain. Storehouses were desperately needed. The transports wanted to be on their way and, as they were costing 10 shillings a day in hire charges, Phillip was equally anxious to see the back of them. By concentrating his resources he was able to get stores built and the provisions were transferred ashore, leading to yet more problems.

Each week the convicts were issued with 3 kilos of biscuits, ½ kilo of flour, 3 kilos of beef or 2 of pork, 2 litres of dried peas and 150 grams of butter. The women were issued with two-thirds of this amount. It was not enough for some. Joe Hall, Henry Lovell and Thomas Barratt had been robbing not only the public store but their fellow convicts, sometimes on the day rations were issued. The three were tried, found guilty and sentenced to death, though Barratt, the leader, was the only one to stand under the gallows, or in their shadow, while Phillip tried to remedy the lack of a public hangman.

Dr White describes the Governor's solution – 'John Freeman was tried for stealing 3 kilos of flour. He was convicted and sentenced to be hanged but while under the ladder with the rope around his neck, he was offered a free pardon on condition of performing the duty of public executioner. After some little pause he accepted.' And after some little help from a bottle of brandy he sent young Thomas Barratt into eternity. It was a sombre reminder that they were on their own.

The transports had left, the *Sirius* under Captain Hunter had returned to the Cape for more grain; if the food ran out, or was stolen, they would quite simply starve. Phillip was prepared to be as harsh as necessary to ensure it did not happen. On one occasion he went so far as to hang six marines who had been systematically plundering the stores. Major Ross was furious. Captain Tench referred to the thieves as 'the flower of the regiment' and passed the affair off as a deadly comedy. To many it was, but the Governor always kept an aim in his mind – Sydney Cove was not just a huddle of huts and tents along the shoreline, it was the future. Phillip had no doubt that one day it would prove 'the most valuable acquisition Great Britain ever made'. Major Ross thought they would have to wait a 100 years before the place was growing enough to feed itself, and it would make more sense for the convicts to dine off turtle soup and venison from the London Tavern.

The spring of 1789 saw a shape begin to emerge from the confusion. Wooden barracks for the marines were moving towards completion; wooden storehouses replaced the stone; a certain amount of lime was being produced from crushed oyster shells (a job for petty offenders) clay had been found in usable quantities and there were hopes of mineral deposits. But as the second winter approached one thought dominated all minds: food. Vegetable gardens had been laid out, but theft had become common. Not a night passed without gardens being looted by convicts and even by the marines appointed to guard them. Choosing the most trustworthy among the convicts, men like Henry Kable and James Ruse, Phillip started a night watch. They were not armed but had power to arrest those out after dark with no legitimate business.

Marines were to be escorted to the guard house where their officers would deal with them. Major Ross fumed that the stopping of a soldier not committing a criminal act was an insult to the Marine Corps which they would not suffer while they had bayonets in their hands. Phillip pointed out that the marines were not above theft. It was not long since six of them had been hanged for it. Ross subsided into a seething silence.

The coastal region would never support crops, that much was obvious to all. Looking to the future, Phillip set up a small farming settlement 10 miles inland, which he named Rose Hill. He placed his servant, Henry Dodd in charge. Dodd had shown a surprising ability both as a farmer and in persuading the convicts in his charge to give of their best. During the second year Dodd and his men achieved a minor miracle of husbandry, but the corn they grew had to be kept for seed and the garden produce, including 26 pounds of cabbage, didn't go far spread around the settlement.

The colony was soon back living off its stores and these were beginning to run out. The last of the butter went, then there were no more shoes and Tench was amused to see the guard parade in bare feet. There was a plague of rats which overran the gardens and stores, and many of the remaining casks of flour were destroyed. The *Sirius* had returned from the Cape, but these supplies were soon used up. Shortly after this, *Sirius* was wrecked on the rocks of Norfolk Island leaving the little *Supply* as the colony's only contact with the outside world.

## The first settlers

The beginning of the third year, 1790, brought a desperate attempt to live off the land or at least out of the bay. On two nights of the week every boat in the colony fished for the common good. Parties of hunters were sent out after kangaroo and emu, but as often as not their blundering through the bush frightened off potential prey.

On one trip they found part of a torn petticoat, hanging from a bush, which was identified as belonging to Ann Smith, the convict girl who escaped as soon as she landed. No other signs were found and it was assumed she had perished. The more simple among the convicts refused to believe this; they were sure China really was somewhere near and bought compasses drawn on scraps of paper which the unscrupulous assured them would guide them to freedom.

Cause for hope was found in the establishment of the first settler, James Ruse, a convict who had served his time. He was given two acres of ground, tools and seeds. Phillip was anxious to know how long it would take an industrious man to become self-supporting. It was no academic question; as the year moved into the rainy season rations were reduced to less than half. This reduced the amount of work that could reasonably be expected from the convicts.

It was a dire situation, and Phillip decided to send Lt King back to England in the *Supply* to impress on the government the need for more aid. As a result, the governorship of Norfolk Island was left vacant and, with a stroke of genius, Phillip appointed Major Ross. The crew of the *Supply*, which delivered him to his new command, added their farewell present by dropping all his possessions into the sea.

At Sydney, 'all our labour,' Watkin Tench said, 'was turned to one object: the procuring of food'. Phillip gave his private stocks to the colony. He did not, he said, wish to see anything more at his table than the ration from the public store. Those who could took a musket everywhere, in the hope of shooting a dinner and if enough was caught to provide for friends. An invitation always read: 'Bring your own bread' and, even at the Governor's table, guests took their crusts from their pockets and placed them beside their plates.

Famine was staring them in the face. David Collins said the expressions of the colonists showed quite clearly their despondency. Tench saw one old man die and when the stomach was opened, it was found to be completely empty. 'Happy was the man who could kill a rat for his dinner.' Most had to put up with the allowance of 50 grams of pork for 24 hours and try to summon up the energy for their tasks. Huge risks were taken by thieves. One man was caught robbing a garden, given a 100 lashes and, while recovering in the hospital, escaped and returned to the scene of his crime, where he was caught again. Lt Maxwell of the marines went insane and rowed himself around the bay for two days before he was brought in.

## The Lady Juliana

June 1790 began with heavy rain. Watkin Tench was in his hut when a confused shouting drew his attention. 'I opened my door and saw several women with children in their arms running to and fro with distracted looks, kissing their infants. I needed no more but instantly ran to a hill where, with the assistance of a pocket glass, my hopes were realized.'

What he saw was the *Lady Juliana* transport entering Port Jackson. Unable to wait, Tench, Collins and Dr White rushed to the cove, grabbed a boat and pulled frantically for the approaching ship. Tench encouraged the others – 'Pull away, my lads. She's from old England. Hurrah for a bellyful and news of our friends.'

The *Lady Juliana* had 200 female convicts on board and supplies enough to restore the full ration. As eagerly awaited as the food was news. They learnt of the French Revolution, of George III's madness and recovery and of a second fleet with a 1,000 convicts due at any time. There was comfort for the marines too. A new Corps was being raised for service in the colony and those who wished to return home would soon be able to do so. For those who stayed there would be land grants and help to set up as farmers.

When the women came off the *Lady Juliana* many were found to be old or sick; once again the authorities had sent out unsuitable material. At times it must have seemed to Phillip that they were trying to sabotage the place. But any disappointment he felt turned to incredulous fury when the second fleet arrived. On the first voyage, under Phillip, there were 36 deaths. On the second, organized on a free enterprise system, there were 280, with 500 seriously ill. The convicts had been kept battened down in their overcrowded and ill-ventilated quarters for the whole voyage. Their rations were so low that on one ship, when men died, their companions said nothing, staying chained to a corpse to get the extra food. Collins visited the hospital White had set up and found 30 tents crowded with people 'labouring under the complicated diseases of scurvy and dysentry'.

The sick were gradually nursed back to health and, with new supplies and greater numbers, work went ahead both at Sydney and at Rose Hill, and during 1791 the pace of settlement increased considerably. Brick and tile storehouses were erected; a more permanent jetty was built for the colony's home-made boat, the *Rose Hill* packet; a play, *The Recruiting Officer*, was put on; licences for the sale of tobacco and alcohol were granted; and a Government House of brick, lath and plaster was built. By the end of the year the wife of a visiting ship's captain could eat kangaroo under its 'hospitable roof' and find it comfortable.

At Rose Hill, renamed Parramatta, more than 200 acres were under cultivation, though there was a setback when Henry Dodd died of a heart attack. James Ruse, the first settler, declared himself independent but continued to draw a ration for his wife.

## Phillip leaves

The settlement was becoming a colony, but the cost to Phillip was a high. His health was deteriorating under the constant strain. He was finding shortages harder to cope with in a detached way and, on occasions, his judgement had become clouded. When a hunting party was attacked by Aborigines, he reversed his policy of friendship and ordered a revenge raid. Fortunately no one was hurt, but it was a bad decision prompted by exhaustion.

At the end of November he requested permission to return to England. He said: 'The settlement is now so fully established that the great labour may be said to be past.' It was and, although months would go by before his request reached London and an answer returned, he had done his job. The little village on Sydney Cove was far from perfect. The newcomer saw a straggle of huts with the odd brick building standing out, muddy tracks, children and animals running everywhere, but the land had been taken and now it would be held.

Phillip returned home at the beginning of 1792. He presented his reports to the government and, after a rest, returned to duty, taking command of the seafencibles, guarding British inshore waters. He was still 'greatly interested in the good of a colony with the establishing of which I have been honoured' but, though his advice was occasionally sought, he was never to see New South Wales again.


## MACARTHUR AND BLIGH

The colony Phillip left behind him had a population of 3,000 which was beginning, willy-nilly, to form a real society. There was little money in circulation, most payments being in kind or in bank drafts drawn on London, but farming was proceeding apace.

Freed convicts were taking up land grants and working with increasing success as they understood the rules of climate and soil. They employed as labourers ticket-of-leave men, pardoned convicts without civil rights who were free to work and choose their employers. This did not suit the officers of the New South Wales Corps, the unit specially raised for service in the colony. Their ideas of how things should be run had nothing to do with convicts improving their lot. They saw Sydney as an open prison with free labour and captive markets, and the history of the 18 years after Phillip's departure is of a continual and bitter struggle between the Corps and the Governors; a struggle, in broad terms, between the state and free enterprise.

'They are soldiers from the Savoy and other characters who have been considered a disgrace in other regiments of the service,' said Captain John Hunter, the second Governor of the colony. The Savoy was a military prison and, though Hunter's judgement was harsh, it was true that many who served in the New South Wales Corps would not have been accepted in any branch of the service where social respectability was of importance. Some joined for adventure, some to escape their debts, but most to make money. The young colony certainly needed entrepreneurs but unfortunately the system was open to abuse and the officers of the Corps would have been less than human had they not taken advantage of their chances.

Phillip left the colony before a successor was named and the administration was taken over by the senior officer at Sydney, Major Francis Grose. Problems soon arose. Joseph Holt, an Irish patriot transported for rebellion wrote – 'It was very provoking to see the officers draw goods from the public store to traffic in them for their own private gains. This was the way those staymakers, tobacconists and peddlers who were called captains and lieutenants made their fortunes.'

Grose was easy going, a stop-gap with no real power or responsibility, and he allowed corruption to flourish more by inactivity than design. He spent no more than two years in office, but in that time he dismissed the civil magistrates appointed by Phillip, ended the fair ration for all and gave land grants to his men with no thought for future needs.

One of the largest, 250 prime acres at Parramatta, had been given to a young captain in the Corps called John MacArthur who had arrived with the second fleet. He was energetic, devoted to his wife and children, industrious and far-sighted; he drank seldom and ate sparingly and was to lay, virtually singlehanded, the foundations of the wool industry in Australia. Yet around him gathered all the conflicts of interest and pride that were to threaten the development of the colony.

At this time though, MacArthur was firm friends with the authorities and Grose even went so far as to appoint him Inspector of Public Works. He performed the task with efficiency and, though harsh, he did not abuse his position, as did many, particularly those involved in the spirits trade. The regiment had become known as the Rum Corps, not because of their fondness for it but for the vast profits they made from its sale. Gin, brandy and rum were cheap to ship, provided quick returns for a small outlay and created an appetite for more of the same.

## John Hunter

The second Governor, Captain John Hunter, arrived in 1795 to find Sydney awash and the Corps in control. Hunter was a decent man, near the end of his naval career, and he found himself out of his depth in the stormy waters of the colony. He saw the public drunkenness and vice occasioned by the trade in spirits, and supported parson Richard Johnson in his efforts to get some decency into social life.

Hunter posted an order commanding all convicts to attend divine service on Sundays at the church Johnson had built at his own expense. A few days later he posted another order – 'Whereas some worthless and infamous person did wilfully and maliciously set fire to the church, notice is given that any person to come forward shall receive a reward of £30.'

No one did. In cases like that, even when the culprit was obviously a convict, the power of the Corps stood behind him. At the centre of the Corps, by virtue of his intelligence and singlemindedness, stood John MacArthur. It wasn't long before he was writing to the Secretary of State in England criticizing Hunter's management of manpower and land and even general life in Sydney. 'Vice of every description is openly encouraged . . . and those whose situation requires the most particular circumspection of conduct are the most openly dissipated.' Unfortunately for Hunter and those who were to follow, MacArthur had a genius for argument and an infinite capacity for causing pain when he thought his interest in the future of the colony was being threatened.

Hunter was nowhere near as singleminded. He could see the need for growth and said that 'if government continues to cultivate land . . . there would be a stop to the exertions of industrious farmers for want of a market for their crops'. But he could not achieve an acceptable balance and in 1799 was ordered home. He said of his governorship, 'I couldn't have had less comfort, though I'd certainly have had more peace of mind, if I'd been in a penitentiary'.

## Philip King

His successor was Philip Gidley King, and his response to the problem was much the same as Hunter's. He was, however, a younger man who had run a successful operation on Norfolk Island and who was not frightened by the task before him. 'I shall have to begin everything anew,' he wrote, 'and must count on having for enemies those from whom I ought to have support.'

He issued an order forbidding officers to buy or sell spirits and stopped the speculators in rum (a generic name for all spirits) from landing their cargoes. In his first year, of the 34,000 gallons which arrived at the cove, 22,000 were sent away. He also attacked the Corps' trading practices by reforming the economy. He realized that this would encourage the growth of a class of emancipated settlers and merchants who would provide the balance Hunter could not find.

Honest weights and measures were introduced, whaling and fishing were encouraged. Prices were regulated and goods sent from England were pegged at cost plus 20 per cent. He also revived the government farms, opened new sites and demanded the return of all free convict labour. In the future farmers and not the government would have to feed and clothe their workers.

He flattered the Corps, becoming fast friends with their new commander, Colonel Paterson, and speaking of their 'soldierlike behaviour . . . which would do credit to the oldest regiment in His Majesty's service'. The general response to this piece of breath-taking hypocrisy is unrecorded, but John MacArthur was not impressed. By 1800, he was worth about £20,000 and owned 4000 acres and 2500 sheep. He was powerful, he was experienced and he was not about to succumb to King's flattery. He knew that the new policy threatened his operations, and the most effective way to counter this was to create an atmosphere of mistrust and suspicion.

A quarrel over a visitor to the colony gave him his chance. Provoking an attack upon himself, MacArthur had the visitor tried by a court composed of his friends. The sentence was absurdly harsh, and when King overturned the judgement MacArthur instituted a boycott of the Governor on all but official matters. He even went so far as to fight a duel with Colonel Paterson who had visited the Governor 'in coloured clothes', that is, socially.

King was furious; Paterson was badly wounded, his life in danger. MacArthur was put under arrest and confined to his property. He demanded a court-martial which he knew would clear him. King refused the bait; he 'judged it necessary and indispensable for the tranquillity of the colony to direct MacArthur to be sent to England'. He also sent a complete resumé of the facts in the case, which mysteriously went missing on the long journey home.

In England MacArthur used his influence to get the charges dropped for lack of evidence. He resigned his commission and devoted himself to the cause of sheep farming in the colony with, as usual, a shrewd eye to his own advantage.

**Sending off the French**
Back in Sydney, King, having got rid of one problem, found himself faced by two of a far more serious nature – the French and the Irish.

In 1796 George Bass, a young surgeon, and Matthew Flinders, a naval lieutenant, had begun a series of voyages to map the outlines of the continent. They were able to establish the existence in the south of straits between Tasmania and the southern coast, a passage which cut 700 miles from the voyage to Sydney

Cove. Bass retired after this discovery, but Flinders was soon off again and during his second voyage encountered a French expedition in the straits which had been named after Bass.

It was a scientific survey but, as everyone in Sydney knew, France was discovering a new imperial purpose under Napoleon, and Baudin, the expedition leader, had given French names to various points and coves along the coast. This was discovered when scurvy forced the French to call at Sydney for fresh supplies. The English received them, as Baudin said, 'with great openhandedness' and resolved to prevent further Gallic incursions.

A small expedition was mounted, Tasmania and the mainland around Port Phillip were claimed in the name of the King and tiny garrisons were left to ensure possession. In one case the Union Jack was planted virtually under the feet of the French who were quite civilized about it all.

A larger expedition was soon mounted under David Collins, the first Judge Advocate. He was to 'waste not a moment' and settle a party of colonists at Port Phillip. He found the excellent soil and thin timber he'd been promised were a figment of someone's imagination and shifted his operation to Tasmania, leaving behind only one man, a convict who was to spend the next 30 years living with the Aborigines. The new settlement was established at Hobart on the river Derwent and the French were frustrated for the time being. The history of Tasmania had begun, though for the island's original inhabitants it was a beginning that would lead eventually to their end.

## Irish revolt
Unlike the French, the Irish could not be sent away. They were in Sydney at His Majesty's pleasure, for political crimes or acts of despair such as cattle-maiming or rick-burning, or for just plain criminal practice.

Governor King was in two minds about them; he had secured a pardon for a transported priest, Father James Dixon, and paid him an annual salary of £10 to perform his office for the benefit of all Catholics in the colony, and yet, at the first hint of revolt or discontent, King responded with the utmost severity. He decreed death for anyone possessing or involved in the making of a pike, and for two people meeting together for more than half-an-hour after being warned by a magistrate to disperse.

Not surprising, then, if the Irish community, which had grown considerably in the 16 years since the first landing, felt resentment and nurtured a hope that here on the other side of the world old grievances might be corrected. To some, like Holt and Father Dixon, the hope was forlorn; change lay in difference directions, through political and religious freedom. Others couldn't wait and on 4th March 1804 a crowd of 200 Irish convicts 'rushed out from Castle Hill. Having seized muskets the whole body came upon the poor settlers, plundered them and threatened their lives'.

When King heard of the rising, he ordered Colonel Paterson to defend Sydney and mobilize troops from any ships in the habour. The rebels, joined by other groups, set off for the settlements on the Hawksbury river where they hoped they would attract more sympathizers. Major George Johnston of the Corps confronted them:

'I rode forward attended by a trooper and Mr Dixon the Roman Catholic priest, calling them to halt, that I wished to speak to them. They desired I would come into the middle of them, as their Captains were there. I refused, observing that I was in pistol shot and that it was in their power to kill me . . . and their Captains must have very little spirit if they would not come forward to speak to me. Upon which two advanced upon me. I called upon them to surrender. One of them

41

replied that they would have death or liberty. I
clapped my pistol to his head and they were both
driven, their swords in their hands, to the
Quartermaster. The detachment formed into a line
and commenced a well-directed fire, which was but
weakly returned, for the rebel line being soon
broken, they ran in all directions. Cunningham,
one of their chiefs, who was supposed dead on the
field, was brought in alive and I immediately
ordered him to be hung up.'

The Governor felt it was a close call and ordered
reprisals – there were several hangings, floggings and
sentences of hard labour at the new coal mines up the
coast at Newcastle. Peace returned to New South
Wales.

And so did John MacArthur, with five precious
merino rams and two ewes. The export of these fine-
fleeced animals was normally forbidden, but
MacArthur had persuaded official opinion with visions
of top-quality wool from New South Wales which would
break the monopoly of European farmers. He had even
got his old enemy John Hunter to support his pleas for
expansion, and on London's say-so he was to have an
extra 5,000 acres and at least 30 convicts to work
them.

Peace was now in his interest. 'Those who were
ready to annihilate one another are now as friendly . . .
as if their whole life had been spent in kind affairs,' he
said, but he could not resist a few dry words on King's
departure in 1806. There had been a terrible flood
along the Hawksbury, a year's harvest had been lost
and the Governor was devastated by the sufferings of
the colonists, many of whom had lost everything.
MacArthur, whose property was untouched, commented
that the tragedy was 'a fine subject for a panegyric on
the care, wisdom and foresight of our friend'.

## William Bligh

King left the colony a disappointed man. His successor arrived full of righteous energy and with the reputation as a fighter the equal of MacArthur. His brief was to impose order and stop the trade in spirits for good. The free settlers saw this as a chance to break down the monopolies of the Corps and begged him, in an earnest address, to ensure their right to an open market and the freedom of trade they had enjoyed under King. The Governor agreed and, while settling in, took stock of his new command.

The population in 1806 was almost 7000, 30 per cent of them convicts arriving on about four ships a year. There were civil and military courts; a growing whale fishery and skinning works, manufactories of linen, sail cloth and coarse blankets. There was brewing from maize and salt was produced for curing meat and fish. Advantages were anticipated from hides, tallow and coal. The biggest problem, the Governor decided, was the attitude of the Corps.

While he considered his moves, they considered him. 'Our new Governor Bligh is a Cornishman by birth . . . he has already shown the inhabitants of Sydney that he is violent, rash and tyrannical. No very pleasing prospect at the beginning of his reign.' Others, including the poor and the orphans of the colony, found him a compassionate man and most of the ordinary settlers supported his reforms enthusiastically.

William Bligh was not one of nature's appeasers; he knew how men should act and do their jobs, and when they failed he could not understand why. 'Remember,' he once wrote, 'I never failed in anything I undertook. I think providence would never have allowed me to have passed so much time among bad people if it had not been for some good end.' Such sublime self-confidence was irritating, and it wasn't long before trouble started, particularly as Bligh wasted no time in stamping on the Corps' business ventures with vigour and success.

There were no deals to be made with the Governor; he considered himself in a state of war with the Corps, and MacArthur was determined to push both parties into a position of no retreat, where the Corps would have to act and take the consequences. It was not difficult to cast a man who'd already suffered one mutiny as a double-dyed tyrant.

## The rum rebellion

A trivial clash, perhaps, but underneath a struggle for power was in progress. Matters came to a head over a schooner owned by MacArthur. The ship had been impounded and MacArthur fined. He refused to pay and a warrant was issued against him by Judge Advocate Richard Atkins, a long-time enemy who was a drunk and a public debtor. MacArthur refused to answer the warrant, calling it a horrid tyranny and voicing his contempt of those who had sent it. This included the Governor and could be seen as sedition. Bligh must have felt that MacArthur had at last gone too far. He was committed for trial, but allowed bail of £1,000.

MacArthur was not idle. He dredged up a 15-year-old bill Atkins owed him and demanded repayment. He didn't get it, which was what he wanted. He then started a squabble over a plot of land he owned within the Sydney town boundary. A number of officers had such plots, granted illegally by Governor King, which Bligh was intent on recovering for the government.

This threat unified the Corps. The night before MacArthur's trial all the officers dined together for the first time since their arrival. MacArthur wasn't present but many of his supporters were, including the six called to serve on the jury. On his way home, Major Johnston, the senior officer, fell over drunk and hurt his arm.

Atkins convened the court the next morning. He took the Bible to administer the oath to himself when John MacArthur made an interruption protesting against him being a member of the court – 'Richard Atkins Esq, my prosecutor in this trial, is so deeply interested in my conviction that should he fail, nothing but the arm of power can save him from prosecution. Now, gentlemen, for God's sake, remember you have the eyes of an expectant public on you, trembling for the safety of their lives, liberties and properties.'

Even in a society which regarded litigation as a public amusement, this was an impressive performance. Nonsense, but impressive enough to galvanize MacArthur's supporters. When he asked if he were to be cast forth 'to the mercy of a set of armed ruffians – the police?' they roared 'no' and took him under their protection.

Atkins reported to Bligh, who summoned Major Johnston. He sent a message that his fall the night before had left him near death and he couldn't write because his arm was bandaged. Atkins and Bligh felt the six officers of the court could well be guilty of treason, a hanging offence. The point of no return had been reached. MacArthur, the Corps and Major Johnston had to act or give themselves up as Bligh's prisoners.

MacArthur wrote to Johnston imploring him to place the Governor under arrest and assume command of the colony. After considerable agonizing, Johnston returned through death's door, rediscovered the power of writing and addressed a note to Bligh – 'Sir, I am called upon to execute a most painful duty. You are charged by the respectable inhabitants with crimes which render you unfit to exercise supreme authority another moment in this colony.'

Leading three hundred men, their colours flying, the band playing 'The British Grenadiers', Major Johnston arrested the Governor. Captured as he tried to burn government papers, Bligh gave no ground and was led away to close confinement, swearing retribution. John MacArthur and the Corps were now in charge of the colony.

## LACHLAN MACQUARIE

Major Johnston set himself up as Lieutenant-Governor and appointed MacArthur Colonial Secretary. Old scores were settled – Bligh's Provost Marshal was sent to the coalmines at Newcastle and Bligh himself was set free on condition he took a ship straight back to England. Instead he assumed command of a Royal Navy frigate visiting the cove and after blockading Sydney went on to Tasmania where he badgered Governor David Collins for aid. Collins, as diplomatically as possible, refused. He had no choice, all his supplies came from Sydney and he dared not offend the authorities, whoever they were.

In London, the government didn't appear unduly concerned. They were involved in a European crisis and had no time for a tiny colony on the other side of the world. Sydney was left to its own devices for almost two years and, in the end, this was perhaps the wisest move. Food supplies dwindled, building work stopped, exploration, farming, paperwork, all were forgotten as a good-natured anarchy overtook the colony.

At last, more by accident than design, London chose a man who was perfectly suited to the task. To heal the rift between civil and military power in the colony, it was decided to install a military Governor with his own regiment to back up his policies. The New South Wales Corps would be disbanded. The regiment chosen was the 73rd, just returned from India, but since its commander was indisposed the office of Governor fell to his deputy, Colonel Lachlan Macquarie.

A Scot in his late forties, a man of noble sentiment and a strong, even overriding sense of purpose, Macquarie was respectable, not much given to humour but deeply concerned with fairness and decency. He was also vain, with a taste for monumental architecture, town planning and bestowing his and his wife's names upon streets, towns, rivers and ranges. His task, as he saw it, would be 'the general improvement of the colony: to reward merit, encourage virtue and punish vice where I find them without regard to rank, class or description of person'.

Johnston and MacArthur were not present to welcome him. They had decided, prudently, to return to London and present their side of the story before Bligh gave his version. The population of Sydney were happy to cheer Macquarie's ship in December 1809 as it sailed through the heads of Port Jackson and into the bay to a salute of 15 guns. Everyone was sick of lethargy, mismanagement and the resurgence of Corps corruption. Even so, the Governor's first proclamation caused a few raised eyebrows:

> 'I recommend a diligent attendance at divine service on Sundays . . . and that marriage should take the place of concubinage . . . and I will direct the constable of Sydney to bring before a magistrate any person that presumes to work on the Sabbath day. . . . And further, all public houses are in future to be shut up during the time of divine service . . . And a very indecent custom having lately prevailed of soldiers, sailors and inhabitants of the town bathing themselves at all hours at the Government wharf. . . . No person shall in future bathe here at any hour of the day.'

Sydney reeled. This was reform on a grand scale; if Phillip had brought Hanover and the age of reason to the south seas, Macquarie seemed equally intent on importing Scottish virtues.

The old Governor, Bligh, was still at sea in his commandeered frigate, calling down the wrath of heaven on his enemies. Macquarie invited him back to Sydney, restored his rank and sent him home to face Johnston and MacArthur on ground more suited to him. Bligh was exonerated and went on to become an admiral. Johnston was cashiered but allowed to return to his farm in New South Wales as a civilian.

MacArthur was beyond military law and, calling on his influential friends, escaped a trial, but, fearing prosecution if he returned to New South Wales, he endured a self-imposed exile of eight years. This, for a family man, was perhaps keener punishment than any judge might have handed down.

## Disturbing the tribes

At Sydney, Macquarie began to implement his revolution of the ordinary man. Joseph Holt, the rebel, wrote that at last 'comfort and happiness began to appear on the countenances of the poor'. Macquarie saw the colony with a double vision – as it was and as it might one day be. He was an improver – of everything.

The architect Francis Greenway, who arrived on a convict ship, was put to work designing noble buildings for a future Sydney where 'the width of the streets will be fifty feet including a footway on either side [and] no person whatever shall erect a house without permission'. To inhabit these spaces Macquarie wanted a population which understood the virtues of self-improvement.

This was an attitude the Aborigines had trouble appreciating. A few still fished in the bay and sold their catch for rum; some even attained local fame, like Bungaree who would welcome newcomers to 'his country'. But the majority kept clear of the settlement for as long as they could. Unfortunately, the settlers didn't return the compliment.

A period of rapid growth had begun and the area under white control kept spreading, upsetting the delicate balance of tribal territories around Sydney. Tribes were driven from their ancestral lands, borders were crossed and violence often followed. A complex form of life was being squashed out of shape and it wasn't surprising that some groups struck back at the invaders, who responded with legislation. 'No body of black natives shall ever appear at or within one mile of any town, village or farm armed with any warlike weapon. No number of natives, exceeding six . . . even being unarmed, shall . . . loiter about any farm.'

Macquarie left no one in doubt about whose country this now was, but 'the fostering hand of time will bring these poor unenlightened people into an important degree of civilisation and instil . . . a sense of the duties they owe their fellows and society in general'. It was the beginning of the Aborigine tragedy, despite Macquarie's good intentions.

## Emancipists and Exclusives

One group in the colony was very much in favour of self-improvement. The Emancipists had become 'by long habits of industry and total reformation' respectable members of the community, but few of them had been received back into society. Macquarie found this absurd. These men and women were deeply committed to the colony, far more than the free settlers who still viewed it as a source of quick profit. To show his support, the Governor invited a number of them to his table – D'Arcy Wentworth, the colony's Chief Surgeon, Simeon Lord, one of its first great merchants and Dr William Redfern, who was instrumental in reforming the appalling conditions on the convict transports arriving in ever increasing numbers.

This elevation of the criminal classes was not popular with the free settlers and officials – or Exclusives, as they came to be known. The Reverend Samuel Marsden had come out to help Richard Johnson with his flock and had ended up with flocks and property of his own at Parramatta, which he ran almost as a fief. A brutal magistrate, he was known as the flogging parson and was not slow to castigate navy and army Governors. 'Neither can see beyond the quarterdeck or the parade ground,' he said. 'They have no relish for the produce of the field.' It was said that Marsden 'had set his face against everything that might help or educate the poor'. He also disapproved of the public amusements Macquarie allowed though they were innocent enough.

The *Sydney Gazette*, the colony's first newspaper, reported horse and trotting races, wheelbarrow races, blindfold running and jumping in sacks. All good clean fun and evidence of a trend towards leisure rather than money-making which was to characterize the nation's development. It was also an indication that the colony was developing into something more than the prison Marsden and his ilk considered the due of those tainted with the stink of the prison house.

## Crossing the Blue Mountains

If the colony's problems were beginning to be those of success, they were none the less serious. The most pressing was the need for space. The colonists were trapped between the coast and the Blue Mountains, a barrier to the grasslands of the interior which no one had been able to cross. In 1813 there was a serious drought in Sydney and a route to the interior had to be found fast.

A party of three, Blaxland, Wentworth (the son of the Emancipist) and Lawson set out and, using the ridges rather than the valleys (a suggestion which may well have come from the Aborigines, who had been crossing the mountains for thousands of years), they made the crossing. Then 30 convicts, under William Cox, an ex-paymaster of the Corps, built a road across the mountains. It climbed over 4000 feet and wound for 110 miles among the sandstone cliffs. It crossed rifts and rivers and summits and was finished in under six months. The convicts who made it got their freedom and the sheepmen of Sydney were given the key to a fortune.

Two years after the crossing of the Blue Mountains, Macquarie granted a charter to start the Bank of New South Wales. Among the first directors were D'Arcy Wentworth and Dr Redfern. Simeon Lord had built a glass works. Francis Greenway had designed and built a turnpike gate, an obelisk, a fountain and a tower. Travellers came from all nations and many were heard to comment on the striking appearance of the town.

## Australia

Everything was changing, even the name of the country. Taking a leaf from the journals of Matthew Flinders, Macquarie dropped New Holland in favour of Australia 'which I hope will be the name given to the country in the future'.

There was also a growing population born in the colony. They were called currency lads and lasses, a reference to the local pound currency which was inferior to the pound sterling, though the lads and lasses felt no inferiority at all:

> 'They grow up tall and slender and generally remarkable for their fair hair and blue eyes. The young men of lower rank are fonder of binding themselves to trades or going to sea, than passing into the employ of settlers. The young girls are of a mild-mannered disposition. They are all very fond of frolicking in the water and can swim and dive like water fowl. The currency youths are all warmly attached to their country, which they deem unsurpassable.'

As always, there were those who felt otherwise, who regarded Australia as an extension of Britain where they would have the power and position denied them at home. The founding of the Bank of New South Wales drew censure from the Colonial Secretary and there were many who felt profound suspicion of Macquarie's liberal ideas.

John MacArthur, back in the colony and enjoying the benefit of the fine flocks his wife Elizabeth had built up in his absence, was not slow to step forward with an opinion. He felt that the business of the colony should be given over entirely to the production of wool and that the control of the industry should remain in Exclusive hands.

It was a view which gained support in London and, combined with righteous indignation over the easy life enjoyed by the convicts, it became heady rhetoric, particularly in the mouth of Grey Bennet, a Member of Parliament with the soul of a popular journalist. He maintained that 'hundreds of persons annually volunteer to go to New South Wales. Not a session passes without the judge being thanked by prisoners for transporting them to Botany Bay'. Most of Bennet's facts came from letters written by Samuel Marsden and were plainly absurd, but Parliament didn't quite fall for Bennet's line. It was beginning to wonder where the colony was heading and where it ought to be heading.

## The Bigge report

A commission under lawyer John Bigge was set up and directed to examine every aspect of life in New South Wales. On his arrival in the colony, Bigge stayed not with Macquarie but with John MacArthur, where he found both the company and opinions much to his satisfaction. The Governor had said – 'This country should be made home, and a happy home, to every emancipated convict who deserves it.' MacArthur's principle, confided to Bigge, was that the country needed a body of 'really dependable settlers, men of capital, not needy adventurers', with estates of at least 10,000 acres. As for the rest of the people, Macquarie's policies would make them jealous of their betters and fractious to boot; best for them to be kept firmly in their places.

It was in the direction of the sheepmen that Bigge recommended the country should go, though without the repression MacArthur advocated. Macquarie had been sent out to protect the settlers and bring the New South Wales Corps to heel. Now those same needy young adventurers who had resigned their commissions and stayed on, had become farmers with fine estates. The growth of wool was what Bigge favoured; there should be increased immigration, with land granted for sheep and convicts employed as shepherds. Britain needed wool, Australia would provide it. As for the turnpikes and fountains, the noble spaces and jumping in sacks, they were of no importance at all.

Predictably the Emancipists loathed the Bigge report. William Wentworth said he had 'raked together all the dust and filth, all the scandal and lies that were ever in the colony'. His feelings were understandable because the report advocated that the Emancipists should lose their restored civil rights. Macquarie had made this the keystone of his administration and, when the report was accepted and enforced, with many respectable citizens losing their rights, he offered his resignation. It was accepted and, to the genuine regret of the colony, 'Australia saw her benefactor for the last time treading her once uncivilised shores'.

Back in England the ex-Governor exerted himself to counter Bigge's recommendations on the Emancipists and, though a sick man, persuaded Prime Minister Peel to revue the Transportation Act and restore their rights and privileges as citizens.

Macquarie had arrived after one revolution and left as another, vastly more important, was beginning. It was sheep which had prompted the crossing of the Blue Mountains; it would be sheep which would spread over the land, pulling the families, the homesteads and tracks, the roads, the towns and cities after them. At the beginning were men like MacArthur but before long those roads were full of thousands of ordinary people . . . small farmers and squatters, diggers, swagmen, the true inheritors of the seeds Macquarie had planted.

# 3.
# THE LUCK OF THE LAND

In 1821 the settlement at Sydney had a population of 38,000. There were 7,000 in Tasmania, but the majority in both places were convicts or Emancipists. Persuading immigrants to endure the discomforts of a six-month voyage and an uncertain future was by no means easy when America, with its settled cities and open plains, was only eight weeks away. But the need for immigrants was pressing.

Britain's population was growing, its agriculture was in recession and European competition was starving its mills and manufactories of high quality wool. It was one thing for Bigge to recommend expansion but it was another to provide the raw material. 'The classes most in demand are shepherds and farm labourers; the trades employed in building; stone masons, quarrymen and lime burners; country blacksmiths, wheelwrights, harnessmakers . . . and a moderate number of tailors and shoemakers,' said an official report, of which there were many.

In the short term the British government decided to provide assistance to workers with valuable trades and free passages to women and girls between the ages of 15 and 30; this was to redress the 'great disparity in numbers' between the sexes. There was no rush for places, but during the 1830s and 40s there was a steady increase in the numbers making their way from farm or cottage, city slum or business house, to the ports of embarkation where, sometimes to the sound of German brass bands and sometimes in silence, they set off on a voyage, often an epic in its own right.

## The immigrant ships

Immigrant ships were generally divided into three, with families in the centre and single men and girls at bow and stern. Discipline on board was strict, administered by the surgeon, a man of considerable importance, whose care and attention could set the tone for the whole voyage. Conditions were often spartan. The Reverend John Davis Merreweather described the single men's quarters on his ship as 'a confused space in the bows. The berths are two deep and have been put up with scant regard for space. The scuttles are blocked up by berths and the whole compartment has a dungeon-like aspect'.

Conditions for families on assisted passages were not a lot better and took little account of privacy. 'There are 48 bed places, six feet by three each, for married people above, and for their children below, each bed place divided from the next by stout planks . . . Tables run the entire length of the ship with fixed seats on each side.' The same space would be used for sleeping, eating and relaxation, with duties such as cooking and cleaning shared on a rota basis.

Cabins and the luxury of privacy were available for those who could afford them. These could also be sure of a warm welcome on arrival for if Australia needed workmen and women, it was desperate for capitalists who could fuel the ecomony. Government was particularly keen to encourage those with £400 or £500, assuring them that their life would be materially better in no time at all where 'labour and capital have now found a working equilibrium'.

The first and worst sea-trial was the sight of land falling away beyond the stern rail. Few of them would see England again. They were committed to their future in a way we would find hard to understand, and the general mood was thoughtful, with not a few tears being shed, as Reverend Merreweather noted at the start of his voyage. He also observed that some young men showed no more feeling than if they'd been going on a pleasure excursion, but as these were the same wasters he'd previously caught 'polluting their quarters with oaths and reading Tom Paine on the infamous Rights of Man', this behaviour didn't surprise him.

There was another class of passenger who had no choice. John Broxup, a Yorkshireman sentenced to seven years for theft, described the routine on the hulk *Retribution*:

> 'Our breakfast was skilly of the coarsest kind and served up in tubs or kids, and as cold as the water that was running around us. There was about half a biscuit. Then there was the inspection to see that we were all washed clean, and such as had a basil or iron on must have this bright. If they were not, or if our stockings had holes in them, we were stopped one penny out of our three pence a week. We did not get the money . . . it was given us in bread. And some never tasted it, for they sold their bread for tobacco.'

The lags found little different on the transports. George Loveless, one of the Tolpuddle martyrs, was put with six others in a berth six foot six square where the prisoners took turns lying down. On the other hand, cleanliness was rigorously enforced after the first few years and sickness took a minor toll. There was scurvy, dysentery and cholera, but no more than 3,000 of 160,000 convicts failed to complete the trip; more of them drowning than succumbing to disease.

**Life on board**
Once the coast was out of sight, life on immigrant ships settled into a routine. There were births and deaths, new companions and strange customs, problems

like sharing a mess with a man who would not wash and had to be given a public scrubbing. There were fights, dancing on moonlit nights, with Scots girls imitating the bagpipes and young Irishwomen vowing to hate the English for ever, There were forbidden assignations, wet clothes and missed meals and, day after day, boredom and discomfort.

Things improved a little in the 1850s when more adventurous masters began sailing the great circle route, covering the distance in one long hop, deep down into the south Atlantic, skirting the pack ice and picking up the roaring forties for the last sweep into Melbourne. On the old route passengers often spent five or six months at sea, but with the discovery of gold and the huge increase in traffic, captains began to make the trip in half the time, driving crews and ships to the limit to shave single days off a voyage.

On occasion there were hints of mutiny. One young emigrant told of a Christmas celebration which turned nasty when the crew mixed with the female passengers and the captain was forced to hold a pistol on them to drive them back to work. On other ships a sailor who so much as spoke to a girl could find himself at the masthead all day while the girl might be confined below for a week or more.

The Reverend Merreweather passed his time teaching the immigrant children the Thirtynine Articles of the Church of England. Others learned to cook everything from rice pudding to sea-balls, or set up mutual improvement societies where they practised addressing letters and public meetings. Gambling was frowned on but the dedicated punter will always find a way as Ensign Best, aboard a convict transport, recalled: 'A convict boy bet four days' allowance of pudding that he would eat the breakfast of eight men – no less than one gallon of oatmeal. He ate it but as it came up again he was under the painful necessity of taking it in a second edition to win his bet . . . which he actually did.'

Food and almost everything else on board connected with the passengers' welfare was under the control of the ship's doctor. His powers were considerable. On one ship the surgeon 'discovered that some of the children have ringworm and that others are covered with vermin. He has given orders that the hair of those afflicted should be cut off. The parents have objected, alleging the appearance of the children will be spoiled, he, however, is inexorable.'

When illness struck, the suffering of the passengers could be terrible, particularly if it was an epidemic and overcrowded hospital facilities reached their limits. The lack of proper ventilation, the constant damp and the movement of the ship, the proximity of young and old and the dying produced an effect that mellowed the heart of even the Reverend Merreweather. 'The emigrants complain sadly of the scuttles leaking,' he wrote, 'their mattresses are saturated with water. They deserve to find Australia an Eldorado, for they suffer very much morally and physically getting there.'

## The 'graduates'

Ironically, the convicts found acclimatization easy. There was a readymade freemasonry, forged in the cities and prisons of Great Britain, ready to receive them; it was rare for newcomers not to find 'graduates from their old schools ready to initiate them into new societies'. The attitude of the authorities was not so welcoming. John Broxup explains: 'After being two days in harbour we were all landed by boat at about five o'clock in the morning and marched to the prisoners' barracks where we were ranked two deep. Shortly afterwards the triangle was brought out, and I counted twenty men who were flogged.'

Newly-arrived convicts were assigned to settlers, often in a lottery with the convict as a prize, as labourers or servants without wages, but, in theory, with their keep and quarters. Others were taken into government service where, though their labour was controlled, they were allowed time to work for themselves and perhaps build a career. On the whole the system was fair and far better than the convicts could have expected back in Britain, but punishment for misdeeds was often terrible. At Moreton Bay in Queensland, at Norfolk Island and at Port Arthur there were prisons for the prisoners where a strict regime met with those who were more than happy to implement it; in those places life was indeed a hell on earth.

Towards the middle of the nineteenth century, the proportions of free immigrant to convict began to alter in all settled areas except Western Australia. The word was getting back to Britain that there was a future in the antipodes, but the increasing flow of immigrants (it would not be a flood until the discovery of gold) made it imperative to find more land.

## THE EXPLORERS

Australia's colonizers had a passion for discovery. Arthur Phillip found relaxation in long exploratory trips, during which he and his companions sampled berries and potentially edible plants with a recklessness which ought to have killed them off, but rarely left them with more than an uncomfortable stomach.

Under Macquarie, the colony expanded across the Blue Mountains and beyond; Cunningham went to north Queensland and Hume and Hovel to the south where in 1824, they pushed through the Australian Alps to the site of present-day Melbourne. They found superb farming land, confirmed in 1836 by Sir Thomas Mitchell who opened up the majority of Victoria: 'the earth seemed to surpass in richness any that I had seen', and he called the area Australia Felix.

One mystery encountered by all early explorers of the south-east was the river system, which appeared to flow west, or inland. There was speculation and hope of the existence of an inland sea or group of 'great lakes on whose verdant banks thousands of cattle might feed [and which might] tempt men to build new cities'.

## Charles Sturt

The first to explore the system was Charles Sturt, an army captain who was born and had served in India and who came to Australia as secretary to Governor Darling. In 1828 he fitted out an expedition inland and discovered a river he named after his employer. The next year he set out again from Sydney, hoping to trace the Darling to its source in the inland sea or to discover an outlet on the south coast. Sturt and his party endured boat-wreck, hunger and thirst and the threat of attack by Aborigines. They discovered 'a broad and noble river' which they named the Murray (after the Colonial Secretary in London) and eventually reached the mouth of the system at Lake Alexandrina, 'a beautiful lake which was ruffled by the breeze that swept across it'. But there was no practicable communication with the ocean and the party had to return the way they had come, nearly 1,000 miles against the current. They rowed 16 hours a day, living on flour and water. One man went insane, Sturt suffered temporary blindness and had to exert all his formidable – some were to say dictatorial – personality to get the party home.

In 1844 he set out again, heading inland where he encountered a climate so hot that 'the horn handles of our instruments, as well as our combs, were split into fine laminae. The lead dropped out of our pencils. Our hair ceased to grow and our nails had become as brittle as glass'. The inland sea, if it existed, evaded him once more; he returned empty-handed but full of stories of the awesome conditions to be met with in the interior. If his adherence to facts was not always of the closest, he did exemplify man's struggle with the continent and show that its massive heart was the ultimate testing ground of explorers.

Edward John Eyre, later to become notorious as Governor of Jamaica, pioneered a cattle route around the Great Australian Bight. He endured all the obligatory torments – hunger, thirst and distance, and the horror of an attack by two of his trackers which left one man dead and Eyre and an Aboriginal companion alone and defenceless. 'Three days had passed since we left the last water . . . 600 miles had to be crossed before we could find help . . . and I knew not one drop of water had been left us by the murderers.' With the help of his companion Wylie, Eyre survived. They became national heroes, or at least Eyre did, though the route they pioneered proved of no real value in linking east and west coast settlements.

**Crossing the continent**
Huge new areas were opened up in the 1840s by Strzelecki and MacMillan in Victoria and Ludwig Leichhardt in Queensland and the north-east. In the north-west George Grey, later to be Governor of New Zealand, surveyed the coast and discovered unique Aboriginal cave paintings.

By 1860 the dream of an inland sea was fading and men's thoughts were turning to the achievement of crossing the continent south to north. Local pride was involved in the young colonies of South Australia and Victoria; both wanted to be first. Their respective champions were John McDuall Stuart, an experienced explorer, and Robert O'Hara Burke, a police inspector and enthusiast who would ride 30 miles to swing on the squeaking gate of a man who annoyed him.

South Australia was prepared to back Stuart to the tune of £2,500; Victoria put up £12,000 for Burke and financed a full-scale expedition (the biggest in the nation's history) with botanists, meteorologists, doctors, surveyors and camels, these in the charge of John King, who had served on the Indian north-west frontier. Unfortunately the instructions were too vague and Burke too human to be a good leader. He would have died for his friends whereas Sturt would have expected them to die for him. Burke, a romantic, could live on good terms with the mystery of the land but lacked the grit and consistency to deal with its deadly tedium. From the moment the monster expedition set out, seen off by the mayor of Melbourne and half the city, it was in hazard.

News came through that McDuall Stuart had begun his crossing from Adelaide and Burke received encouraging messages: 'It will be to a certain extent a race between you and him – now I know how exciting this must be to you . . . and now will come the time of trial for your coolness and caution.' They were not qualities for which Burke was renowned. Many of the members of the expedition found his leadership intolerable. There were many reasons – jealousy, his nationality, perhaps the way he dribbled into his beard, his lack of experience in command and the triumph of heart over head. Those who supported him were generally younger men, lacking experience and vanity, like John King, the camel handler and William Wills, a surveyor.

The expedition set up a base camp at Menindee, the last settlement before the unknown. Here Burke reorganized, getting rid of surplus stores and appointing Wills as his second-in-command. Rather than wait out the hot season – and risk McDuall Stuart getting there first – Burke set off with eight men for Cooper's Creek, 400 miles away. This was to be the final jumping-off point for the crossing. Wills noted that 'the rats attacked our stores in such numbers that we could keep nothing from them, unless by suspending it in a tree'. He was fascinated by everything, which was just as well since Burke had left all his other scientists and experts, including the doctor, back at the base camp.

**Burke's mistake**
Once at Cooper's Creek Burke split his party still

further, leaving four behind with instructions to build a stockade and await the arrival of the main party. He set off with Wills, John King and Charley Gray, an ex-sailor who had the reputation of a capable bushman. Burke told those who were to remain: 'I shall be back in a short time. If I am not back in a few months you may go away.' They had a horse and six camels and 1,500 miles of unknown country ahead.

They followed the straggling waterholes of the creek to the area known as Sturt's Stony Desert. They crossed this and joined the Diamantina river, then followed Eyre's Creek, where they found evidence of Aboriginal occupation including piles of empty shells. Wills noted everything down because Burke found 'it impossible to keep a regular diary, I shall just jot down my ideas when I have an opportunity.'

By the end of January 1861, six months after leaving Melbourne, the four had crossed the Selwyn mountains and were into the tropical north, where they found no relief from the damp heat day or night. The ground underfoot was almost impassable and it was decided, on 10th February, to leave the animals in camp with Gray and King while Burke and Wills made a dash for the coast, which they all felt was close.

Aided by a party of Aborigines who pointed out directions, the two 'reached an extensive marsh, at times flooded by sea-water. Hundreds of wild geese, plover and pelicans were enjoying themselves'. Though they could not see it, they had reached the Gulf of Carpentaria. There was an eight-inch tide in the marsh and only their lack of provisions and the bad ground stopped them going further. Burke wrote: 'It would have been well to say we reached the sea, but we could not obtain a view of the open ocean, though we made every effort to do so.'

**Tragedy**
They now had to return to Cooper's Creek. They had been gone 57 days and had used more than two-thirds

of their provisions. They had also driven themselves
relentlessly and, now the rainy season was setting in,
they realized how exhausted they were. Day after day
it poured. They had no tents and were still in the damp
heat of the tropics. Night-travelling avoided the worst
of the climate, but there were other hazards. On 3rd
March, when crossing a creek by moonlight, Charley
Gray rode over a snake, eight feet in length and seven
inches in girth. They killed and ate it; two days later
Burke, already weak, suffered a serious attack of
dysentery.

After 40 days they re-crossed the Selwyn range. They
were no more than halfway back and things were
falling apart. On 25th March Wills wrote, 'I was taking
some time-altitudes and on going back to the camp . . .
found Gray behind a tree eating some of our stores.'
Gray explained he was suffering from dysentery but
Wills was in no mood for excuses. He reported the
matter to Burke who, in the spirit of a *Boy's Own*
adventure gave the unfortunate man 'a good
thrashing'.

Day after day, night after night they trudged on,
their clothes in rags, the freezing desert nights sapping
their energy. They killed animals, drying the meat into
leather-hard strips which they chewed, but the lack of
a balanced diet was causing serious problems. They
had dumped all inessential items as they re-crossed the
Stony Desert, but they were deeply overdrawn
physically and approaching bankruptcy. On 17th April
Charley Gray died of exhaustion. The survivors were
now 70 miles from Cooper's Creek and, after burying
Gray, they pressed on, covering 12 miles a day and
ignoring the Aborigines who observed them with
detachment. By 21th April they were within 30 miles
of the creek. Calling on their last reserves, they pushed
through the night.

They arrived to find that they had missed the base
party by less than eight hours. Some food had been left
but no clothes. The base party had been forced to leave

by inefficiency: they had not been re-supplied in the whole time Burke was away. Apart from dispatching a confused word-of-mouth message before setting off, Burke had worked out no system of support and supply. Now he and his companions were to pay for it.

'The exertion required,' Wills wrote, 'to get up even a slight piece of rising ground induces a sense of pain and helplessness. Poor Charley Gray must have suffered many times when we thought him shamming.'

They couldn't stay at the creek, because of the lack of supplies. There were two possible routes back: to follow the footsteps of the other party and head for the base camp 400 miles away, or to make for Mount Hopeless, 150 miles distant, where there was a police post and the land was more settled. Burke favoured the mountain, though Wills disagreed, and they set off in that direction, at first keeping near the waterholes of the creek and then striking out, hoping to find the water they no longer had the strength to carry.

Every route they tried was dry, and they were constantly driven back to the creek, getting weaker each day. The last animals had died, and they could only wait for rescue, surviving on the nardoo flour cakes the Aborigines had shown them how to make from local plants. On 12th June Wills noted: 'This nardoo will not agree with me in any form – but we are now reduced to it alone . . . it cannot possibly be nutritious enough to maintain life by itself.'

John King and Burke made one last attempt to find the Aborigines who had left the area. Alone in camp Wills wrote: 'I am weaker than ever. Nothing now but the greatest good luck can save any of us. As for myself, I may live four or five days.' Burke too was near the end. Unable to go on, he collapsed, addressing his last words to John King: 'I hope you will remain with me until I am quite dead. It is a comfort to know that someone is by. But when I am dying it is my wish that you should place the pistol in my right hand, and that you leave me unburied as I die.'

After Burke's end King returned to Cooper's Creek where he found William Wills dead too. He buried him and went in search of the Aborigines. When he found them, they showed great compassion and he stayed with them for two months until a rescue party arrived.

An inquiry followed. There were questions, evasions, blame was placed and shifted and nothing of consequence was established. What Burke, Wills, King and Gray had established was not so much a route from south to north – though within a few years sheep and cattle were driven along it – but a sense of what was possible and what the price might be.

## Uluru

Burke's great rival, McDuall Stuart, completed his route in 1862. Shortly afterwards South Australia assumed administrative control of the lands he'd surveyed, which were known as the Northern Territories. Others followed, striking into the west away from the established lands, uncovering portions of the vast central emptiness. In the 1870s, W. C. Gosse found the sacred monolith the aborigines called Uluru. He named it Ayers Rock. Ernest Giles discovered the Olgas, a strange, isolated mountain range in the middle of nowhere. He went on to discover, in a series of epic journeys, more than any other man about the interior. On several occasions he faced death alone; once, on the verge of starvation, he found a baby wallaby and 'pounced upon it and ate it; living, raw, dying – fur, skin, bones, skull and all.' It is hard to imagine Robert Burke showing such passion for survival, but by romantics or realists the continent was being opened for the settlers and their dreams of a better life.

## THE LAND

Settlement had spread so fast from the original 13 counties around Sydney that some scheme of land distribution would obviously have to be found. There were a number of choices.

One of the most persuasive came from Edward Gibbon Wakefield who considered Australia from an English prison cell to which he'd been sentenced for the abduction of an heiress (the second he'd abducted). His ideas were a logical answer to a nagging problem: how to encourage immigration, call a halt to uncontrolled land grabbing and provide workmen where land could be had for the asking and labourers were nowhere to be found. He suggested a system that would allow 'the people to exert their utmost capacity for doubling themselves but no more', and this was to be achieved by selling grants of land rather than giving them free, thereby creating a wage economy. The money raised could form an immigration fund to provide assisted passages for more workers, who would do seven years or so as labourers before stepping up in their turn.

Wakefield's ideas were tried in various forms and with varying success, but as Britain's industrial appetite increased, the scramble for land became as frenzied as in any of the later gold rushes. Banks offered unsecured loans on the hint of good grazing just over the hill; big farmer or small, a man could expect to double his flocks and holdings every two years. It was a boom time and to meet the needs of the new arrivals expansion began on all fronts.

## Tasmania

Tasmania, first settled in 1804, had grown steadily both as settlement and prison. In the early years it had suffered from bushrangers, escaped convicts who terrorized settlers, but under Governor Arthur the economy began to flourish.

A dour puritan, Arthur ruled the settlers much as he ruled the convicts under his charge. Citizens dreaded his receptions which lacked decent food and civility; the Aborigines of the island had even less cause to appreciate his virtues. Under his rule the notorious hunt was mounted for the last of the natives. A line of beaters, extending across the whole island, walked steadily forward with the intention of gathering their prey like fish in a net. The scheme did not work. Only a young boy and a sleeping woman were captured, but the white action was to have deadly consequences both in Tasmania and on the mainland.

## Western Australia

In 1829 Captain Charles Fremantle landed on the west coast at Arthur's Point, where he took possession of all land not previously claimed by Great Britain, securing one-third of the continent in one sweep. The settlement he founded was to be free of convicts and cheap labour. Behind the scheme was Thomas Peel, a cousin of the British Home Secretary, who was given a grant of 250,000 acres along the Swan river in recognition of his expenses in setting up Australia's first private colony.

Things did not go smoothly. 'Five times as much land was disposed of in one year as was got rid of in New South Wales in forty. Upwards of a thousand labourers were sent out but the extravagant prices for labour furnished them with such facilities and inducements to become landowners', that there was no one left to hire. This was the situation Wakefield's minimum price for land was supposed to remedy, but the Swan river's problems were compounded by distance. They were simply too far away . . . from their own mineral wealth, from the markets of the east and the trade routes, which were building such cities as Melbourne. The only answer seemed to be transportation, just as the other colonies were agitating to have it stopped. In the long run, convict labour helped Western Australia survive into a secure future.

## Victoria

The colony of Victoria had no such problems. Its land was above average, good for grazing and growing and was settled without any prompting from government.

John Batman formed an association, purchased 600,000 acres around Port Phillip from the local Aborigines (it was a beads-and-blankets deal) and put down his roots. Others, like Thomas Henty and his family, originally from Sussex, moved across the straits from Tasmania. By 1840 Melbourne was well established and boasted over 10,000 inhabitants. Within the next 10 years, when Victoria separated from New South Wales, Melbourne became 'a city with somewhere between 20 and 30,000 inhabitants, possessing many buildings, sending forth mail coaches and steamboats daily to . . . Sydney and Hobart town. In Melbourne there are extensive stores where every luxury and necessity may be procured . . . and the country behind Geelong is now in the course of settlement for sheep runs and is extremely well spoken of.'

## South Australia

South Australia was founded in 1834 as the result of Wakefield's theories. It was privately financed with the aim of creating a farming state for pious dissenters. The scheme was not a great success until George Gray arrived as Governor in the 1840s. He increased taxes, reduced government spending and encouraged squatters in their search for new land.

Valuable mineral deposits were discovered, but the greatest advantage, shared to some extent with Victoria and New South Wales, was the Murray-Darling river system which provided 4,000 miles of navigable waterway from the Queensland border to the south coast. With the coming of steam, the river currents which had hampered earlier travellers were no longer a problem and goods could be transported quickly and at low cost. In the 1830s Colonel George Light founded Adelaide which, within 20 years, had a population of 14,000 and became the centre of a state which, perhaps as a legacy of its early ideals, has always had the reputation of being forward-looking.

## Queensland

Queensland was felt to have and perhaps still has different qualities. Growing from the harsh convict settlements of Moreton Bay, its progress was slow at first, but after separation from New South Wales in 1859 (the name suggested by Queen Victoria) its population began to grow. The discovery that the climate was perfect for sugar cane and that the South Sea islands provided an abductable labour force (the practice was called blackbirding) provided the springboard for the state's future wealth.

## The squatters

The squatters who populated these young colonies were of all sorts, from the selectman with his small property and not much more than he carried on his back, to the young man with money to invest and adventure on his mind; from the political refugee to the family with their servants and possessions. Not all came from Great Britain; there were some from mainland Europe, who found in their new country, and particularly in South Australia, a freedom undreamed of in the old. 'In Europe upheaval, religious hatred, partition, fury, revolution among all the nations; here, peace, the plough, the sciences, the founding of new cities.'

Many of the younger squatters were aware of their dashing reputation, and were happy to live up to the image of the devil-may-care adventurer who could not exist without his horse, rode 50 miles every day at the gallop, fought hordes of Aborigines, ate raw emu and slept with his saddle as his pillow.

The reality was something else. It was a hard, lonely and often dangerous life with no doctor to attend accidents or illness and always, always the land to contend with. Edward Curr describes driving his sheep to market:

'I started for Tongala with 2,000 ewes. The summer, for it was the month of December, was hot and dry and at Mount Gamal my sheep got their last drink. The distance to Tongala was about 55 miles. Crossing the plains I remember took two days and a half of tedious driving, the sheep being in one lot with two shepherds. As a matter of course we had a bullock dray with us on which we carried, among other things, a cask of water for us and the sheep dogs. The bullock driver, who was a cantankerous, bad-tempered fellow, refused one time to allow the men to drink from the cask. This irritated them not a little and occasioned a row at our midday camp which ended with me sending the driver about his business.

Towards sundown we arrived at Tymering, and camped among the she-oaks. The whole party was a good deal fagged, as our drive of eight miles, which was all we could accomplish, was over treeless plains under a burning sun, so that nothing but the most constant efforts on our part could keep the sheep moving. It was Christmas eve, I remember, and a furious hot wind had been blowing the whole day in our faces. Weary, begrimed, half choked with the dust, with bloodshot eyes and sunburned faces, the three of us sat at the camp. The mournful wailing of the wind and our fatigue made us disinclined to talk, so we sat in silence.

In the distance quantities of peculiar red-coloured bushes were rolling away to the southward, tumbling over and over before the gale. No birds were to be seen, but here and there moving columns of dust, grass, leaves, the result of whirlwinds, towered high in the air; while close at hand, covered with ashes from the small fire which, though lately kindled, had already burnt itself out, lay our kettle, frying pan and the bag containing our gritty meat and damper. To

complete the scene there were the panting sheep
and bullocks with protruding tongues; the close on
setting sun bathing the landscape in a dull red
light, suggestive of an eclipse.'

The bullock driver sent away by Curr was a member
of the most important trade of all in the opening of the
country. Everything that couldn't be manhandled was
hauled by bullocks, which worked harder and pulled
more for less feed than horses. Yet even they were
expensive, and all but the most valuable loads were
carted at low profit and high cost. Often it was cheaper
to import from Europe or America to the coastal cities
than to send goods the last few hundred miles inland.
The bullock drivers, the bullockies, gained a reputation
as hard bitten hellraisers in moleskin breeches and
cabbage-leaf hats, cursing their way across the hardest
terrain, flicking flies from the ears of their oxen with
15-foot bullwhips. In parts of the outback they were
still delivering the necessities of life in the 1890s, and
Jeanne Gunn, in her account of life in the Northern
Territories, says it took a good six months' hard
driving to supply a year's goods to three cattle and two
telegraph stations.
   Drought and the economic vagaries which produced
slumps were things no one could foresee and the
progress of the squatters was by no means a smooth
ride. During the early 1840s a credit squeeze forced
prices down, and overstocked farmers boiled down their
sheep by the thousand for tallow. In one year over
750,000 were destroyed, and many saw 10 or 20 years
of back-breaking work gurgling out of the tap as white
fat. Some failed but more survived and, as new systems
of land leasing were introduced, the economy took an
upturn. Fundamentally, the young country was in good
economic shape and the slump was soon forgotten.
Success was in the air for those who worked.

## Mates

There was one problem that all the sheep in Australia
couldn't solve; the lack of marriageable women. This
was in spite of a policy encouraging women to emigrate
and the work of Caroline Chisholm, whose Female
Immigrants' Home was designed to protect newcomers
from exploitation. During the 1830s men outnumbered
women by three to one. By the 1850s this had dropped,
but not in the bush. The facilities for raising families
were in the towns and cities and it was there the real
growth of the country was taking place. A squatter
might be able to support his wife and children, even a
servant or two, but the men he employed as shepherds
or stockmen could not offer a settled existence to
anyone.

Men lived a solitary life in the bush, dependent on
one another for everything; it was from this that the
tradition of mateship grew. Good times, bad times,
everything was shared, everything paid for and never
stolen. Trust had to be absolute if the decencies were to
be maintained. Because of this unrelenting struggle,
tenderness and care could be shown without loss of
face:

> 'And though he may be brown or black,
> Or wrong man there or right man,
> The mate that's steadfast to his mates
> They call that man a white man.
>
> They carry in their swag, perhaps,
> A portrait and a letter –
> And maybe, deep down in their hearts,
> The hope of 'something better'.
>
> Where lonely miles are long to ride,
> And long hot days recurrent
> There's lots of time to think of men
> They might have been – but weren't.'

So wrote Henry Lawson, whose brilliant short sketches were to sum up so much of the unyielding world of the squatter. At times, out on the sheep runs or driving the herds to the small, sedately-growing towns, it must have seemed as if the country was so set in its ways that nothing would ever be changed.

## GOLD AND RIOT

In mid-nineteenth century Europe the last few years had been a time of revolutions; in France, Austria, Italy, Hungary and the Slav states. All were crushed. Everywhere the old order had been restored, but in Italy Garibaldi had begun his fight to unite the country and in Germany a young Jewish thinker, Karl Marx, had published a pamphlet which would become known as *The Communist Manifesto*. In Russia millions of serfs were still owned and would stay that way for another 11 years, In the United States the slaves had 14 years to wait for freedom and in Brazil nearly 40. In China the British had forcibly established their right to sell opium to the people. In London the Duke of Wellington had died and the Crimean War loomed. The safety match had been invented; people were reading Charles Dickens's new monthly magazine and the huge glass palace which was to house the Great Exhibition of Britain's imperial power was near completion.

### Gold!
Australia . . . was waiting. Perhaps for Richard Hargraves, who arrived from the goldfields of California and decided to apply his experience to the eastern coast.

He set out from Sydney with a companion, heading for Summerfield Creek near Bathurst, where the geology looked right. He dug a pan of earth, washed it and produced a small nugget of gold. He washed another five panfuls and found gold in all but one. He said: 'This is a memorable day for New South Wales. I shall be a baronet, you shall be knighted and my old horse will be stuffed and put in a glass case in the British Museum.'

The pair had discovered what swagmen and squatters had been finding for ages: a small, unprofitable surface deposit, but it suggested that workable deposits could be located. There was no baronetcy or stuffed horse for Hargraves, but he was able to persuade a grateful state government to award him £16,000.

At first the news of the find was not made public. The country was still recovering from the slump of the 1840s and though local officials had no experience of gold finds they could imagine what the rush of men from settled work might do to the economy. Three months later the *Sydney Morning Herald* let the news slip out in its domestic column. Common sense vanished as thousands left their jobs, bought prospecting equipment, the blue and red serge shirts and Californian hats all the shops seemed to be selling, and headed off convinced that a couple of days' work would see them rich.

Gold was discovered in Victoria five months later, in June 1851, by James Esmonds, another graduate of the California goldfields. Worried by the drift of population across its border, the government had offered a prize for any gold found in its territory, but success created other problems. The state was newly formed, and right from the beginning faced a budget deficit and complaints from the farmers and squatters who packed the new legislature. They were opposed to the loss of labour and the rising cost of goods and working men, and blocked state attempts to set up and finance new goldfields.

In addition, the rush of imports to service and tempt the miners was upsetting the economic balance. In one year the cost of carting goods to the fields was over three million pounds; but if the rush was expensive, ill-organized, undisciplined, it was nonetheless a rush towards huge rewards. Where there was gold to pay, there would be goods and services to sell.

Freeman Cobb, an American, adapted the light well-sprung Wells-Fargo coach and, by changing his teams every ten miles and employing American drivers who were forbidden to drink on the job, he was able to provide a fast and efficient transport system. It was needed, for once the news reached Europe and America the rush became a tidal wave heading for the ports of Victoria and New South Wales.

In 1852 over 86,000 left Britain for Australia, and most of them paid their own fares. They were going to be diggers, not farmers, and their fortunes were lying just beneath the ground at Kalgoorlie, Bendigo and Ballarat . . . names rapidly assuming mythical status. For the Americans it was a return engagement, because many of the Australian diggers had been to California where the rowdier elements were known as the Sydney Ducks. In fact, before the building of the Panama Canal it was faster and easier to travel from San Francisco to Sydney than to New York, and it wasn't long before Old Glory was flying over the goldfields as well as the Union Jack.

### The diggers
The main problem for the state governments was to create order from the confusion. Disorder and violence reigned and a whole sub-culture was built up around the diggers.

Inns were forbidden on the fields, though this didn't stop the *sly-grog* sellers who created a good deal of trouble with their illicit products, trouble more often than not settled on the spot by the diggers who had their own notions of trial and sentencing. A visitor to Victoria reported:

'. . . hearing the sound of an angry crowd. We hurried to the spot and found that summary vengeance was . . . being inflicted upon an individual who had been caught plundering a tent. His face was already covered with blood, his shirt torn open. Women were shrieking, men shouting and dogs barking. Some were for lashing him with a rope's end, others for drowning him. [In the end] the poor fellow had his back whaled with a half-inch rope in such a manner as will make him remember as long as he lives the justice of a crowd.'

The gold which brought these people together was found in two forms. On the surface, in alluvial beds, it was gathered by cradling; under the ground, combined with quartz rock, it was reached by sinking shafts between fissures. It was these shafts, sometimes sunk hundreds of feet to the deep veins or leads of gold, that provided the big finds, the sudden fortunes, but the work was harder and more dangerous than surface scraping. In muddy ground the shafts need constant draining and the sides had to be shored up with slabs. At Ballarat, one party sunk a shaft 90 feet and in a few days realized £12,000, but the mine was badly slabbed. Rather than risk further work, they leased the digging to a more experienced group who, between Saturday and Monday morning, dug a further £8,000 worth of gold.

The vagaries of chance tended to create a feeling of equality among the diggers; luck could lift a man today and throw him down tomorrow. Learning, class, political influence had little to do with the luck of the land, and this characteristic suspicion of ready-made credentials became an abiding part of the national character. 'There are no gentlemen in the colonies now. All barriers are broken down. There are only rich men and poor men; and as the latter may be rich men in a week, everyone is "hail fellow, well met" with everyone else.'

The fortunate diggers would return to the towns and cities to relax, Melbourne's population of 20,000 rose to over 80,000 in a month. It was a boom town: 'The bars were always full, the taprooms always crowded. The women as numerous as the men. Wedding parties without end drove up and down the streets by way of cutting a flash.' There were endless calls for another round of neat whiskies or Old Toms and Nobblers. At the theatres, some concocted from shanty shops, others wonders of gold leaf and velvet plush, successful diggers thought nothing of throwing nuggets wrapped in £5 notes to performers who pleased them – or rocks at those who did not.

## The licence

The government in Victoria or, what amounted to the same thing, the squatting influence, had different concerns. As forecast, labour costs had risen; who would be a shepherd or a milliner when they could be a millionaire? The forces of law and order were also suffering from wholesale desertion to the diggings, and the attempted solution of this problem was causing even more trouble. A number of ex-convicts from Tasmania had been drafted into the police force by the Governor and though many were honest, others were not above a little bribery and corruption. Police or police spies were allowed half the value of fines levied as a result of their information. Not a recipe for good police-public relations.

Another sore point, not unconnected, was the checking of miners' licences; spot checks with a fine for any who could not produce their documents. Raffaello Carboni, an Italian digger, reported:

'One fine morning I was hard at work and I hear a rattling noise among the brush. "What's up?"
"Your licence, mate," was the peremptory question from a six-foot fellow in blue shirt, thick boots, the

face of a ruffian, armed with a carbine and fixed
bayonet.'

One of the reasons for the licence system was to get
idlers off the goldfields and back into ordinary
employment. This pleased the legislative council, but
they refused to vote funds for the proper
administration of the fields. For their part, the diggers,
with no representatives to put their view, began to
agitate for reform. The Governor, La Trobe, desperate
for some kind of revenue, contemplated doubling the
licence fee to £3 per month. Protest escalated.

On the fields there was an extraordinary spirit of
libertarianism and bloody-mindedness – born of gold
and its power and English chartism, Irish nationalism,
Yankee republicanism and European socialism of half-
a-dozen different hues. There were near riots, mass
meetings and demands. The diggers had the example of
New South Wales across the border, where the licence
fee had been cut. This was eventually forced on the
Government of Victoria, though it had none of its
neighbour's economic advantages. In August 1854 the
fee was reduced to £1. the original plan of revoking it
altogether was blocked by the squatters, who made
their dissatisfaction so plain that Governor La Trobe
was replaced by Sir Charles Hotham.

Balancing the budget and stopping the waste were
his first tasks. He was a believer in democracy and
visited the goldfields to see the diggers' problems and
hear their point of view. Wishing to please, the diggers
put on a show, plucking nuggets literally from the
ground for the Governor's inspection. One was
presented to his wife. It must have seemed as if the
whole field was bursting with wealth, though in fact
the diggers had seeded the gold themselves just before
Hotham's arrival. Not unnaturally, he decided that if
gold was that easy to pick up, there was no reason why
a colony facing bankruptcy shouldn't be saved by these

wealthy miners, He ordered the goldfield commissioners to step up their checks on the monthly licences.

At Ballarat, the local commissioner, Rede, was sympathetic to the digger's complaints, but found himself forced to increase the hated checks, relying on a police force and local magistrates more than a little tainted with corruption. Various newspapers began to support the diggers and it wasn't long before local leaders emerged.

### The miners' leaders

One was Frederic Vern, an ex-soldier from Germany 'with the eyes of an opossum, a common nose, not very small mouth, long neck for Jack Ketch, broad shoulders never broken down by too much work, splendid chest, long arms . . . a lion among the fair sex in spite of your bad English, worse German and abominable French.' Rafaello Carboni, the fair-minded chronicler of the goldfields, was anything but a lion – though he had red hair. He was a good if idiosyncratic linguist, a dubious ex-revolutionary and something of a self-publicist.

The best known was Peter Lalor, an Irish engineer in his late twenties. He was the son of an MP and, though one of his brothers had been active in the struggle against England, Peter was a man of peace. He had been well educated and was politically a conservative but, like so many of his countrymen, he had a fine understanding of the way governments may oppress. He had been in Australia two years and, after working on the construction of the Melbourne railway, was trying his luck on the goldfields.

The Americans at Ballarat needed no encouragement to stand up for their rights. James McGill, a 21-year-old digger, formed the Independent California Rangers Revolver Brigade. Carboni commented, 'They looked Californian enough, armed with a colt's revolver of a large size, and many had a Mexican knife at the hip.'

There were also a few English chartists looking for peaceful changes but their voices were lost as the mood of the goldfields hardened.

In October 1854 James Scobie, a friend of Lalor, was involved in an argument with a shady hotel owner, Bently. Later, on his way home with a friend, Scobie was attacked and kicked or battered to death by Bently. The friend escaped to spread the news and Bently was brought up before the magistrates, some of whom were involved in corrupt dealings with him. Bently was freed. The diggers were furious and gathered in front of his hotel, which was protected by a squad of police troopers. Bently was inside, but not for long. He escaped on horseback, heading for the government stockade. The crowd went wild and burst through the cordon 'and in a moment furniture, bedding, drapery, curtains, sheets are tossed out of the window. The weatherboards are ripped off the sides of the house and sent spinning in the air'. Someone applied a match to the bowling alley next to the hotel. 'More troopers arrive, but too late. They form a line in front of the hotel, swords drawn. Hurrah, boys! No use waiting any longer. Down she comes. Police try to extinguish the flames – it is too late – hip hip hurrah is the universal shout . . . the roof and the back part of the hotel fall in. Hurrah, boys! Here's the porter and the ale with the chill off!'

Within days the Governor had 400 police and military on the field. Four diggers were arrested at random and released immediately by the magistrates who had decided not to push their luck. Bently was then arrested together with three more diggers. They were held while Bently was tried, found guilty and sentenced to three years. The local police were examined and discredited, the three miners were found guilty of riot. A delegation from the fields arrived to see the Governor. They demanded, though without threats, the return of their three convicted companions. This was impossible, they were told, but a commission to inquire into the state of the goldfields would be set up. It was too late.

### Eureka stockade

A detachment of the 12th regiment on the way to the fields was stopped by armed diggers. A wagon was overturned and ammunition stolen. Peter Lalor counselled calm. Carboni thought otherwise. 'We are compelled to demand and must prepare for the consequences.' Frederic Vern, the ex-soldier, demanded that all diggers should burn their licences. Proposals were adopted – full and fair representation, manhood suffrage, no property qualification for membership of the legislature, disbanding of commissions and abolition of licence tax.

The next day a small government force entered the field, and asked a miner for his licence. The digger ran into a crowd of his mates. They closed around him. Commissioner Rede read the riot act, but nobody heard him. He faced his troops about and commanded them to fire a volley above the heads of the crowd. Stones were thrown in return.

Peter Lalor heard the noise and hurried to the scene. The soldiers had taken up a position behind a log barrier. The miners procured a flag, the Southern Cross (designed by Charles Ross, a young Canadian), showing the constellation of that name in the form of a cross, silver on blue. Lalor and the others waited for one of the accredited leaders to stand up, but no one did. Lalor felt '. . . the grievances under which we had long suffered, and the brutal attack of that day flash across my mind and, with the burning feelings of an injured man, I mounted the stump and proclaimed: Liberty.'

An oath was taken and the rebels gathered arms and built a protective stockade at the Eureka diggings. By Saturday, 2nd December, three days after the meeting, nothing had happened and the men were beginning to drift away to eat or see their families. Those who remained were mainly Irish. During the afternoon McGill and the Revolver Brigade arrived but soon left to cut off government reinforcements which were heading for the fields.

That evening about 150 men were sleeping at Eureka when nearly twice that number of soldiers and armed police approached. They launched their first attack at first light. The soldiers were using new French rifles and their fire was devastating. Though the diggers fought well and fiercely, they could not stand for long. Charles Ross was shot dead beneath the flag he designed, Peter Lalor was hit in the shoulder. Fires were started and the police were not slow to settle old scores:

> 'Here begins a foul deed worthy of devils. The accursed Troopers were within the stockade. They deliberately set in a blaze all the tents around . . . the howling and yelling was horrible. The wounded are now burnt to death; those who laid down their arms were kicked like brutes and made prisoner.'

It was short, bloody, doomed . . . and unnecessary. When Governor Hotham's commission reported, it recommended that all the demands of the Eureka men should be implemented, and they were. The goldfields returned to normal within days, public opinion firmly settled on the diggers' side.

The Americans involved were not prosecuted; the government did not want to offend the United States. All 13 diggers indicted, including Carboni, were freed. Peter Lalor lost an arm but escaped prosecution and went on to a career in public service. Twenty-three diggers and five soldiers died, but the symbolic nature of the incident – men taking up arms against government corruption, the creation of the flag, the rhetoric and the songs – made a small incident on one goldfield another necessary link in the forging of a nation.

# 4.
# WITHIN OUR OWN SHORES

Australia was heading towards nationhood, just as its people were moving from the bush to the cities. It was the beginning of the age of mass movements – political, social and economic. The long age of the individual was coming to its end.

Victoria had separated from New South Wales in 1851. Queensland was founded in 1859. These colonies, together with South Australia and Tasmania, had achieved parlimentary government based on the British system. There were two houses, a lower called the Legislative Assembly, and an upper, the Legislative Council. The Assembly was elected by the votes of all men in the colony, the members of the Council were either appointed by the Governor or elected by large property holders. There were a few matters of Imperial concern which Britain controlled, and the final assent to Australian bills had, of course, to be given by Queen Victoria, but from 1856 to 1894 only 32 were held up and eventually all but five were passed.

Not that the state parliaments always ran smoothly. An observer wrote: 'New South Wales, South Australia and Victoria have had, respectively, 28, 42 and 26 ministries in 40 years. The policy of the opposition has often been identical with that of the government. In some rural areas candidates appeal to the electors on personal grounds.' And again: 'A chimney sweep who shouts for popular liberty here would get in before a sound man with some conservative leanings.'

Without hereditary interests and power blocks – apart from the squatters – politics were more open and liberal than in Britain. But parliamentary democracy still had to find whether its roots lay in the bush and the farms or in the towns and cities where the majority were settling.

The shape of the goldrush had changed by the mid-1850s. There were far fewer individual diggers on the big fields; the remaining gold, and there was still a lot, was buried deep. Planning, surveying and deep-shaft mining were necessary and the companies with capital were taking over. They employed only a fraction of those who had settled on the diggings. The rest, the thousands who had flooded into Victoria and New South Wales, had to find alternative work. For some that meant a life on the land, but the majority saw their future as far as possible from the loneliness and hardship of the bush.

## The new cities

The cities they went to were of all sorts. Adelaide in the 1850s was a well planned and pleasant town with 'many neat villas, with handsome gardens and cool verandahs', and an auction mart which would have been considered 'an ornament to any English town'. Melbourne, Marvellous Melbourne, had expanded at a terrific rate, becoming the capital of what was, in effect, one of the richest states in the world. Farming and gold had allowed the town to outstrip Sydney in growth and influence and in culture too, though many home-grown artists complained of the 'Titians' and 'Raphaels' which arrived from abroad at surprisingly reasonable prices.

There were bound to be problems in accommodating the rush of settlers, and areas developed similar to those to be seen in the industrial cities of Europe. On

the steep slopes to the west of Sydney Cove a district
known as The Rocks was:

> '. . . occupied by several so-called streets running
> longitudinally. There are also cross lanes or
> passages, the ascent of which is sometimes
> facilitated by steps. These streets are not roads,
> being scarcely traversable by vehicles, and
> destitute of all signs of forming, metalling,
> guttering, sewering. The houses are small and
> ancient stone cottages. Where the erections are of
> wood, their dilapidated, filthy appearance is all
> the more striking. The interior of these abodes
> usually consists of two dirty, bare, rusty-coloured
> chambers, of small size and yet too large for the
> scanty articles which constitute their furniture. In
> many cases the foul drainings of one cottage
> trickle down the hill till they encounter the front
> or back wall of the house below. Here they
> accumulate, soaking in at the foundations or
> sometimes passing in at the door. In some houses
> the occupants have prevented this by constructing
> a drain close beneath the floor, running through
> the house. Certainly a flowing stream of filth is to
> be preferred to a stagnant pool. The various
> rejectments of more solid nature which lie about
> the yard and streets where they chance to fall, of
> course add to the foul appearance and smell.'

This was perhaps exceptional but, as populations
grew, resources began to break down. A report on city
conditions in the 1860s stated that the streets of
Sydney were:

> '. . . infested by a large number of vagrant children
> entirely neglected by their parents; and some of
> the revelations of juvenile depravity are appalling.
> According to an officer of the Metropolitan Police,
> the traffic in female prostitution has extended its

meshes around unhappy children scarcely above the age of infancy. The number of boys in a vagrant state is variously estimated, but the evidence shows that a large class exists to whom the possession of parents is of no value in giving direction to their lives. They are floating about the streets and lanes like fish in a pond.'

## The selection experiment

In the bush things were often little better. To provide for the landless from the goldfields, the system of free selection was introduced during the 1850s. This allowed up to 320 acres to be bought with a down payment of 25 per cent, the rest to be paid, without interest, within three years. The only stipulation was that the land be used for crops. The big sheep and cattle farmers loathed the little men who took up valuable grazing land. And for those selected, caught between the banks and the climate, life was often brutually hard. Henry Lawson describes such a farm:

'Spicer's farm was a big dark humpy on a patchy clearing, fenced in by sapling poles resting on forks and x-shaped uprights. The dusty ground round the house was almost entirely covered by cattle dung. There was no attempt at cultivation, but there were old farrow marks among the stumps of another shapeless patch in the scrub . . . The hut was nearly as bare inside as it was out – just a frame of round timber covered in bark. The furniture was permanent, unless you rooted it up: a rough slab table on stakes driven into the ground, and seats made in the same way. The beds in the bag and bark partitioned room were simply poles laid side by side on cross-pieces supported by stakes driven into the ground, with straw mattresses and some wornout bedclothes. The plates and cups were of tin, there were two or three cups without saucers, also two mugs, cracked and without handles, one with 'For a Good Boy' and the other with 'For a Good Girl' on it. But these things were kept on the mantleshelf for ornament. They were the only ornaments in the house save for a little wooden clock that hadn't gone for years.'

Only in South Australia was the selection experiment a success, building on the foundation of arable farming and the Lutheran industry of the German settlers. Over the rest of the country the scheme was a failure, a fact admitted only in the 1880s, when a hungry, discontented rural class had come into being.

## English and others

Where organization was possible in the cities, there was a struggle for an eight-hour working day. The masons, with their vital skills, began the movement in the 1850s. They formed a labour league and joined others, including carpenters, bricklayers and slaters (all important in an expanding economy). The workers presented a demand for 'Eight hours work, eight hours recreation, eight hours rest and eight shillings a day'. They achieved this in Melbourne in 1855. Sydney soon followed and over the next 20 years the movement and the demand spread around a country which had no entrenched conservative tradition. Australian civilization was, as one commentator put it, 'English . . . with the upper classes left out'.

For those who weren't fortunate enough to be English, the outlook was not so rosy. The Chinese, as prone as anyone to the lure of gold, had been arriving throughout the 1850s and by 1857 there were more than 40,000 in the country with only four or five women of an inferior class among them, as a Select Committee reported. A tax of £10 was imposed on each Chinese immigrant but this was often evaded, not by the law-abiding Chinese but by the merchant captains who brought them from Hong Kong and landed them at deserted coves and bays along the coast. The Chinese would gather there in groups of 500 or so and set off for the goldfields in processions which wound, snake-like, for miles across the countryside.

They were met with suspicion, prejudice and often outright hate. They were not a useful addition to Christian society and where, the moralists wondered, were all those men going to relieve their sexual needs – was this the beginning of the end for Australia's fair daughters? Apparently not, though the anxieties of many white miners overflowed into action at Lambing Flats in Victoria in 1861. A group of 3-4,000 attacked the Chinese shanty town, where tents and stores were destroyed, butchers' shops burned down and mining equipment smashed. The miners then set off after the Chinese who had retreated to Back Creek. Some 1,200 'unarmed, defenceless and unresisting were struck down in the most brutal manner by bludgeons and pick handles. The wretched Mongols were openly . . . searched for valuables and robbery was committed without the slightest attempt at concealment. Very few of the poor creatures escaped with their pig-tails – none without injury of some kind.' The reporter finished his description with the thought: 'Who among the British people could ever believe that men of their own country would take Chinese pig-tails . . . with the scalp attached.'

In time heads and tempers cooled. The riot was an isolated outburst but reflected a deeper and growing concern in Australia about its Asian and Oriental neighbours.

The Chinese were, at least intentional immigrants. The islanders of the Pacific, from the Solomons, New Hebrides and Fiji, were tricked or kidnapped by blackbirders and transported to Queensland, where 60,000 of them laboured in the canefields of the colony. The profit for the owners was massive and, in a state beginning to feel its potential, there was no question of stopping the practice. In 1883 Queensland even attempted to annex eastern New Guinea, not only for the extra labourers it might provide but because of a general feeling in Australia that if London wouldn't secure it for the Empire (and it wouldn't), Australia must.

The British were not impressed with this precocious imperialism. Mr Gladstone muttered: 'I suppose Queensland to be untrustworthy as well as unauthorized.' The British Governor of the state added his opinion:

> 'New Guinea would be placed directly in subjection to the council of a comparatively uneducated community which has shown itself notably regardless of the commonest rights of humanity in respect of the black native tribes within its own territory, to say nothing of what has been disclosed of the trade in sugar workers.'

Queensland was forced to pull out and Germany, whom Britain had been concerned not to offend in the Pacific, claimed the northern half of New Guinea. Britain had no choice but to occupy the south-east and conclude an Anglo-German treaty. Australia was not pleased. Many maintained that had the country 'spoken with one voice', and had that one voice been of a federal government, New Guinea would not have been lost.

## The cable link

One voice which was being heard across the continent was the telegraph. The London-Sydney cable link, via Java and Darwin, had opened in 1872 with the final meeting of the overland telegraph. 'At one o'clock the government received a message direct from port Darwin, intimating that the last length of the wire had been stretched and that uninterrupted communication across the continent had been established.'

South Australia had financed and built the overland cable, 2,200 miles of wire stretching across the outback and linking isolated stations like The Peak, Beltona and Alice Springs, named after Alice Todd, wife of a superintendent of telegraphs). The link was vital (though contact was often easier between nations than between states), and the construction a great achievement, but the work did not end there. The unending task of checking the line was important.

Jeannie Gunn and her husband lived on a cattle station in the Northern Territories:

'One of the earliest of our guests that year was the telegraph operator who invited us to "ride across to the wire for a shake hands with the Outside", and within an hour we came in sight of the telegraph wire as our horses mounted the stony ridge that looks over the Warloch Ponds . . .

For a moment we waited spellbound in the brilliant sunshine, then the dogs ran down to the water's edge, the galahs and cockatoos rose with gorgeous sunrise effect – a floating grey and pink cloud backed by sunlight flashing white. But the operator, being unpoetical, had ridden on to the wire and presently was shinning up one of its slender iron posts as a preliminary to the handshake, for tapping the line being part of the routine of a telegraph operator, shinning up posts is one of his necessary accomplishments.

And as we stood, in touch with the world, in spite of our isolation, a gorgeous butterfly rested for a brief space with gently-swaying purple wings, and away in the great world men were sending telegrams amid clatter and dust, unconscious of that tiny group of bush folk, or that Nature, who does all things well, can beautify even the sending of a telegram.'

## Feeling the way

A greater stir was caused in some quarters by the Secular Education Acts passed by all the states during the 1870s. There had been little religious tension in Australian history since there was no official religion and no church subsidies. The problem had arisen when the states cut off aid to church schools.

The Roman Catholics, who used their own text books and had priests as teachers, felt this was directed mainly at them. Since the early years, Catholic congregations had become more respectable and better off and their bishops did not hesitate to speak out, but to little effect. Idealism in the country was harnessed to the pursuit of material rather than spiritual benefits, and while men might suffer for the eight-hour day, the Secular Education Acts went through without much opposition.

'To some degree the workers of all the Australian colonies possess advantages which make Australia a worker's paradise. High wages are combined with cheap food and leisure for culture and amusement.' But Sir Charles Dilke's view at the end of the 1880s contained a little wishful thinking – many were still working a 70-hour week – but there was no real doubt in the minds of most people that they were living in a prosperous land where the future would be claimed by hard work and good luck.

The country was beginning to wonder how it would deal with the rest of the world, politically and economically. Protectionism had long been practised in all the states except New South Wales, but on the political front, though most Britons assumed federation to be inevitable, Australian feelings were not so clear. A large proportion of public opinion felt the British fleet could play an important part in dissuading any who might say, 'Here is a large part of the world you are not using . . . make way for somebody who will.'

Britain was at last coming round to the view that the Australian colonies represented good value. During

the 1870s and 1880s British investors had put over
£250 million into Australian industry. The London
*Times* was moved to say: 'With the colonies massed
around us, we can hold our own in the ranks of world
powers. Without them we must sink to the position of a
merely European kingdom.' The real storms over
federation were to come in the 1890s. The country was
still feeling its way, testing new doctrines and ideas
against old problems and hopes.

## White Australia

Industrialization and the growth of mining was
creating a new working class with no long traditions
behind it, which was able to discover its own
aspirations more easily than its European brothers and
sisters and utter them with greater freedom. Writers
like Edward Bellamy (*Looking Backward*) and William
Lane exerted an immense influence on young
Australian socialists, though there were one or two
discordant notes in the generally harmonious melody:

> 'Australia is not a sect or section, it is not a cast
> or class or a creed, it is not to be a southern
> England nor yet another United States. Australia
> is for the whole white people of this continent, and
> the policy is the continuance of that
> enlightenment which has already proved her,
> while still in the colonial stage, foremost among
> the states of the earth.'

Working men's associations, from the Chartists
onwards, have never been averse to kicking the other
fellow, especially if he is foreign, or worse, foreign and
a different colour. William Lane, Utopian Socialist,
later to found a colony in Paraguay, was no exception.
'We must be white in order to keep our white
civilization. Our children must be white in order that
they may take the lamp of progress from us and keep it
burning for the generations to come.'

In 1878 white seamen went on strike when their employer took on Chinese labour, and the union movement supported them, as did the country at large. By 1885 laws had been enacted to render Chinese entry to Australia virtually impossible. There were fears that increased immigration would flood the job market, which would be disastrous for the young unionmovement. There were also a sense of unease about the Chinese and their culture, hazy notions of racial purity and, above all, questions about who might be in control of the country in 200 years' time.

## NED KELLY

In 1855, the year of responsible government, a man was born in a shanty outside Melbourne who came to exemplify the virtues and vices which the rest of the country feared might soon be lost under the new responsibility. His name was Edward Kelly.

'Take no offence . . . if I take the opportunity of writing a few lines to you. It seems impossible for me to get justice without I make a statement to someone that will take notice of it . . .' He was a tireless writer of letters and excuses and sometimes of threats. His messages and exploits ensured that his name is known by every contemporary Australian child.

He was the son of a bush carpenter, Red Kelly, who died when Ned was 12, leaving a widow, Ellen, and four other children. Times were hard. The rich squatters of Victoria had no time for those selected for land grants, and the police were on the side of the big money. Among their standing instructions was, 'Without oppressing the people or worrying them in any way, you should endeavour, whenever they commit any paltry crime, to bring them to justice and send them to Pentridge Prison, even on a paltry sentence.'

By the time he was 20, Ned had served two prison terms and ridden with a local bushranger. The experience was to prove useful. After a second prison

sentence of three years for horse stealing, he found his
attempts to go straight frustrated by his reputation
and by constant police harassment of his family.

In 1878, Dan Kelly, Ned's 16-year-old brother, was
accused of stealing a saddle. He was acquitted on
producing a receipt, which may well have been forged,
but a local police trooper, Constable Fitzpatrick, would
not accept the verdict. He paid the Kellys a drunken
evening visit. In one of his letters, Ned described what
happened:

> 'On the fifteenth of April Fitzpatrick came to the
> Eleven Mile Creek. He went to the house – asked
> was Dan in? Dan came out. He said he had a
> warrant for him. Dan then asked him to produce
> it. He said it was only a telegram. Dan's mother
> said he need not go without a warrant and the
> trooper had no business on her premises without
> some authority besides his own word. The trooper
> pulled out his pistol and said he would blow her
> brains out if she interfered. She told him it was a
> good job for him Ned was not there – or he would
> ram his revolver down his throat. Dan looked out
> and said "Ned is coming now" – the trooper being
> off his guard looked out and Dan slipped Heenan's
> Hug on him and took his revolver, and kept him
> there. When the trooper left he invented some
> story to say he got short – which anyone can see is
> false.'

It was, but that did not deter the jury. On
Fitzpatrick's evidence, they convicted Mrs Kelly and
two neighbours giving her three years and them six
months apiece. Dan escaped and, with two friends,
Steve Hart and Joe Byrne – neither strange to the
criminal world – joined Ned in the Wombat Hills. They
were followed closely by four mounted policemen who
caught up with the outlaws, as they now were, at
Stringybark Creek.

Ned's bushranging experience stood him in good stead and he was able to surprise them. One of the troopers ran for his horse, mounted and shot at Ned. Ned killed him before he could fire a second shot. Another trooper ran and the gang let him go. The other two were shot down:

> 'Lonigan ran . . . to a battery of logs . . . and put his head up to take aim when I shot him that instant, or he would have shot me. Kennedy ran . . . I shot him in the armpit and he dropped his revolver. I fired again as he slewed around to surrender . . . the bullet passed through the right side of his chest and he could not live or I would have let him go.'

The 23-year-old outlaw was a cool hand with a revolver and a sight more deadly than his opponents. He said he was sorry for the widows and children of the police but:

> 'I have been wronged and four or five men lagged innocent and is my brothers and sisters and mother not to be pitied also who has no alternative, but to put up with the brutal and cowardly conduct of a parcel of big, ugly fat-necked wombat-headed big-bellied magpie-legged narrow-hipped splay-footed sons of Irish baliffs or English landlords which is better known as Victorian police.'

## Jerilderie

There was no going back. A price of £1,000 was put on the head of each of the young outlaws. There were no takers, even in a district of utter rural poverty no one would try to claim the reward, though many knew where the outlaws were.

The gang held up the bank at Euroa, taking £2,000, then took over the town of Jerilderie in New South Wales for several days. The police were locked in their own gaol or escorted around town by their captors. The bank was locked and the mortgage records burned; the telegraph was put out of action:

> 'We were standing in front of the telegraph office, when a man came charging across the street and pulled up his horse at the fence. I said "That's Hart!" and walked inside. He passed the postmaster, stopped at the telegraph forms, put his hand in his pocket and pulled out his revolver, and told us to close. We then went outside and met Ned Kelly. We proceeded to the Royal Hotel where we saw a whole crowd of people trying to look as if they relished the joke.'

When the gang went, Ned left behind a long letter detailing the history of his struggles and putting his and his family's viewpoint. Flushed with the success of the raid and the popular support he was receiving (though the townsfolk were unlikely to criticize him to his face), he ended:

> 'I give fair warning to all those who has reason to fear me, to sell out and give £10 of every hundred towards the Widows and Orphans Fund and do not attempt to reside in Victoria but as short a time as possible after reading this notice. Neglect this and abide by the consequences, which shall be worse than the rust of the wheat in Victoria or the drought of a dry season to the grasshoppers in New South Wales. I do not wish to give the order full force without giving timely warning, but I am a widow's son outlawed, and my orders must be obeyed . . . Edward Kelly.'

Jerilderie was in New South Wales, which had always looked down on the cabbage-patch state of Victoria. Now here were four Victorian bushrangers getting clean away with a daring and stylish raid. The authorities, stung, pursued the band relentlessly.

## Siege of Glenrowan

It was only a matter of time for the outlaws, and Ned
must have known this by the end of 1881. The gang
had lain low for 18 months, during which they had
fashioned armour from ploughshares. They had also
executed an associate, Aaron Sherrit, who was in
contact with the police. Joe Byrne shot him, in front of
his mother, beside his 15-year-old wife, saying, 'I have
come down to take Aaron's life. The bastard will never
put me away again.' Byrne and Sherrit had been
childhood friends, and the betrayal was keenly felt, as
was the revenge.

The gang retreated to the town of Glenrowan, which
they took over, and waited for the inevitable arrival of
the authorities. A posse, lead by Superintendent Hare
soon arrived by train. Night was falling and the gang
was holed up in Jones's Public House. Without waiting
for the innocent to escape, the police began blasting.
The outlaws fired back and for 15 minutes the night
was shattered by gunfire and the muzzle flashes of
revolvers and rifles. After this outburst, things settled
down into a siege, with occasional shots being
exchanged. Then just before dawn a scream echoed
from the pub. It was Mrs Jones 'lamenting the fate of
her son who had been shot in the back, she supposed
fatally'. She emerged, crying bitterly, and wandered
into the bush.

Shortly after dawn the police allowed out the rest of
the women and children. They were checked
individually in case one of the gang was trying to
escape in disguise. Then silence fell and the police
waited for the final engagement, but when it came
they were again surprised. From the mists of the bush
a strange figure approached the rear of the police lines.
Clad in a long grey coat, wearing his famous helmet,
Ned Kelly walked slowly forward, taking his time to
aim and fire as the hail of police bullets whined off his
body and head armour.

For a moment it seemed that this apparition might

turn the course of the battle. Ned rapped on his breastplate with his pistol and called to the others, 'Come out boys, and we'll whip the lot of them.' The police, collecting themselves, began shooting at his arms and legs and he fell, shouting 'I am done, I am done.' He had been shot in the left foot, left leg, right hand, left arm and twice in the groin. He lay, conscious, glaring at his captors while the attack on the hotel continued.

By afternoon the shooting had stopped, but rather than risk a frontal attack the police set fire to the building and waited. No one came out. At great risk, a priest ran inside and found the bodies of Dan Kelly and Joe Byrne side by side. Each had a pistol in his hand. The bodies were burnt almost beyond recognition. Joe Byrne's body was propped against a wall for press photographers and sketch artists to record. A crowd gathered around Ned Kelly who said; 'I could have got away last night, for I got into the bush with my grey mare, and I lay there all night. But I wanted to see how the thing ended. The bullets that struck my armour felt like blows from a man's fist. I expected the police to come . . .'

### Trial and execution

He was taken to Melbourne and tried at the Central Criminal Court. A defence was offered but there could be no excuse. Kelly was an angry, confused young man whose family had traditionally regarded the police as enemies. When he and his family were harassed, he struck back and felt it natural to do so. Kelly was no 'assassin or killer', his counsel said, 'on the contrary he had proved himself to have the greatest possible respect for human life'.

The jury needed only half-an-hour to bring in the guilty verdict. The judge asked if there was anything the accused wished to say before sentence was passed. There was of course:

'I dare say the day will come when we shall all have to go to a bigger court than this. Then we will see who is right and who is wrong. As regards anything about myself, all I care for is that my mother, who is still in prison, shall not say she reared a son who could not have altered this charge if he liked to do so.'

The judge replied:

'The end of your companions was comparatively a better termination than the miserable death which awaits you. It is remarkable that though a large reward was offered for the detection of the gang, no person was found to discover it. There seemed to be a spell cast over the people of this particular district.'

Sentence of death was passed, ending with the traditional words, 'May God have mercy on your soul.' Ned replied, 'Yes, I will see you there.'

Efforts were made to procure a pardon. Mass meetings, a petition with over 60,000 signatures, a letter from Kelly to the Governor, but the execution went ahead. Ned's mother was allowed to see him and told him to die like a Kelly. Which he did. Beneath the gallows he said, 'Ah well, I suppose it had to come to this.'

### The legend born
There was no other possible end to Ned's life, but this was just the beginning of the legend. At first it reflected the dreams and hopes of the poor squatters of Victoria, mainly Catholic, for a future where they would have a real say in public affairs. There was even talk, among the most passionate, of a breakaway Catholic republic. This didn't happen but as Irish-Catholic influence spread, Ned's legend rode not on his old grey mare but on the advance of Catholicism to

equal status in society. Nowadays he is a national
hero, an individual in an age of conformity, a free-
ranging murderer in a law-abiding world.

During the 1880s there was a growing realization that
Australians were fortunate people. They could buy
products ranging from continental bicycle tyres to
rustless corsets; maternity and child benefits were just
over the horizon; their standard of living was as high
as any country in the world and far better than their
parents would have known in Europe.

Their relationship with the country, the struggle to
come to terms with its hardships, was seen as a source
of justifiable pride. Papers like the *Sydney Bulletin*
were beginning to advocate nationalism, which had
nothing to do with looking back to Old England for
leadership. Indeed Britain was seen as the oppressor of
'the gallant Scots' and the 'enslaved and downtrodden
Irish', who made up a larger proportion of Australia's
population than did the beef-eaters.

In Melbourne there were both Imperial and Native
Australian Associations, highlighting a split which was
going to deepen as the years passed, though, with
typical humour, many Australians were members of
both. Alfred Deakin, an architect of federation, enjoyed
the facilities of both without detriment to his career.

Australia was becoming a place where people and
organizations fitted together, where there was room for
differing opinions in the general consensus; however,
there were still the old fears of Asia, and British
treaties with the 'nigger Empire' (India) were not
looked on with approval. The unions had other
problems; the boom-and-bust cycle of economic growth
during the nineteenth century was about to turn from
the good years to the bad.

## Strikes and slumps
All over the world, the last years of the century saw a
slump in output, bank failures and drops in wool and

wheat prices. Australian producers reacted by lowering wages. The unions would not stand for this, so the employers turned to non-union labour:

'The price of wool was falling in 1891
The men who owned the acres saw that something must be done,
"We will break the shearers' union, and show we're masters still
And they'll take the terms we give them, or we'll find the men who will."
From Clermont to Barcaldine, the shearers camps were full;
Ten thousand blades were ready to strip the greasy wool;
When through the West like thunder, rang out the Union's call –
The shed'll be shore union, or they won't be shore at all.'

So ran a ballad of the time in support of the shearer's strike, rapidly followed by industrial action in the zinc and copper mines at Broken Hill. There were riots and bloody clashes – in one of which the officer commanding the troops gave the order to 'fire low and lay 'em out'. Fortunately such attitudes were rare, though there was a celebrated case at Rockhampton where strikers were gaoled.

The strikes were broken but the struggle planted a new idea in the minds of the unionists:

'It was a spirit of altruism, of sacrifice, of faith, of white hot enthusiasm which animated the Labor Party. Self-seekers and time servers, men consumed by ambition, passed it contemptuously by on the other side for its hosts were ragged and its camps bare. But it was in deadly earnest and imbued with a passionate resolve to right the wrongs the few had inflicted on the many.'

The slump hit Australia hard, and the depression everywhere was appalling:

'The Government was powerless to deal with the tragedy of unemployment. The country districts swarmed with men seeking work and, for the lack of it, demanding food at the squattages and selections. Many establishments are not more than paying expenses and the proprietors merely continue working in the hope that a revival will take place. It is particularly unfortunate that business is so bad at the present time, as reducing wages means a curtailment of the purchasing power of workmen, and rents and other expenses will have to come down in consequence, but employers declare they cannot pay the present rates and that the only alternative is to shut their establishments entirely.'

## Federation
Many saw federation as a way out, as an expression of national identity and a potential support in hard times. The six states (the Northern Territories were still administered by South Australia) were virtually separate nations, with their own railway gauges, postal systems, social legislation and trade laws.

The Intercolonial Conference of 1883 had voiced concern over French and German incursions into the Pacific, and a Federal Council was set up to examine a possible national response to these threats. Due to squabbles between the states, it produced nothing, but further impetus was given towards federation in 1889 when a British soldier, Major-General Edwards, reported on the defensive capacity of Australia.

He wrote, 'No general defence of Australia can be undertaken unless its distant parts are connected with the more populous colonies in the south and east of the continent.' Looking to Europe, where the recently unified Germany was intent on colonial expansion, he warned that because 'it is the unforeseen which happens in war, the defence forces should be placed on a proper footing; but this quite impossible without a federation of the forces of the different colonies'.

Shortly after this report, the Premier of New South Wales, the flamboyant Henry Parkes, began publicly supporting the cause of federation:

> 'The Government of New South Wales is anxious to work in harmony with the governments of the sister colonies. We believe the time is now ripe for consolidating the Australias into one. Why should not an Australia be equal to a Britain? But there is something more. Make yourselves a united people, appear before the world as one, and the dreams of "going home" would die away. We should have "home" within our own shores.'

There was general support for the idea but the Federation Conference of 1890 was no smooth ride. Western Australia, which had just struck gold, wanted to retain its independence. New Zealand had no intention of sheltering under the Australian umbrella. Electoral setbacks occurred, but the idea was planted in the nation's mind and needed only time.

Alfred Deakin, who was to become the country's second Prime Minister, said, 'To those who watched the inner workings of the ideal of federation, and lived a life of devotion to it day by day, its actual accomplishment must always appear to have been secured by a series of miracles.'

The setbacks of the referendum of 1898 were to prove temporary. In June 1899 the country voted 70 per cent in favour of federation. Western Australia held aloof for only nine months before joining the rest of the states. Delegates travelled to London and thrashed out the details with Joseph Chamberlain who informed the House of Commons:

'We have come to an absolute agreement. This leaves Australia absolutely free to take its own course where Australian interests are solely and exclusively concerned. I hope the bill will be passed unanimously and I fully believe that the House may pass the bill with the full conviction that in sanctioning the Union of Australia they have in no way impaired or weakened the unity of the Empire.'

The Commonwealth of Australia was officially inaugurated in Sydney on 1st January 1901. The city was decked with flags; a huge parade wound its way through the streets, passing under triumphal arches of coal, stone and flowers, many presented by individual sections of the community like the Chinese citizens or the Germans. Others bore congratulations from the nations of the world: 'The United States welcomes United Australia.' There were brass bands and soldiers in scarlet and gold, 'two thousand little girls all clad in white shook two thousand handkerchiefs at the dragoons and lancers'; there were Cabinet ministers and Death or Glory Boys from Victoria; there were reporters and artists and photographers and thousands of ordinary Australians, quite happy to see their taxes spent on a public show. The cry was 'One people, one destiny.'

No one asked the Aborigines to join the celebrations.

## Parliament and policies

Parliament was opened by the Duke and Duchess of York. It was presided over by a Governor-General and consisted of a lower House of Representatives and an upper Senate. The lower house was to be elected every three years, its membership proportional to the state's populations. The less populous states were compensated with six places each in the Senate.

Australia's first Prime Minister was Edmund Barton. His government called itself Liberal, which meant nothing very much at that time, when most of the running was being made by the emerging Labor Party. By 1903 they had a firm programme, including old-age pensions, the nationalization of monopolies, the principle of a citizens' defence force, and the maintenance of a White Australia Policy. This had always been a strong plank in Labor's platform, and was shared by every other party. To implement it, the dictation test was set up: any immigrant unable to write 50 words in a European language would be refused entry to Australia. W.M. Hughes, a Welshman who'd arrived in the 1880's and pursued a political career with a mixture of passion and personal ambition, pointed out that *he* hadn't spoken English until he was eight years old, so what was to stop an educated Japanese from learning the language:

'. . . and it is above all the educated Japanese that we fear. There is no conceivable method by which they, if they once get a fair hold in competition with our own people, could be coped with. If the higher class of coloured men come in, the educational test will be swept aside by men who can learn anything in half the time which a European needs to acquire.'

With this and other more worthy policies the Labor Party went from strength to strength, but not everyone was convinced of their socialist credentials. Lenin said:

'In Australia the Labor Party is purely representative of the non-socialist workers of the trade unions. The leaders of the Australian Labor Party are trade union officials, an element which is everywhere most moderate and capital serving, and in Australia is altogether peaceful and purely liberal.'

Not all was peace. The country had sent a contingent to South Africa during Britain's Boer War, assistance which may well have eased the path of the federation bill. It was during this adventure that two Australian soldiers, Harry ('The Breaker') Morant and P.J. Hancock, were executed by a British firing squad. Morant, a colourful character who had published verses in the *Bulletin*, was accused of shooting a prisoner-of-war in revenge for the killing and mutilation of a comrade by Boer commandos. On being sentenced to death, he refused a blindfold and told his executioners to 'shoot straight and don't make a mess of it'. Opinion in Australia was not best pleased by what it saw as an example of British hypocrisy. Legislation was passed ensuring that no Australian would be executed in future without a thorough investigation and express permission from the federal government.

**The arts and sport**
On the whole, the early years of the century were a period of experiment and social change. In 1907 the principle of a basic wage was laid down in law by Mr Justice Higgins. It was estimated that a labourer's household of five people needed 32 shillings a week. The basic wage was set at 42 shillings. This ruling precipitated a rush to join the unions, which helped them to recover from the defeats of the 1890s. There were also moves by small, local organizations to combine and take advantage of federal measures.

Australian art and culture was trying to escape from the influence of Britain, and though thousands waited at the docks for the latest news of Little Nell, many more were trying to come to terms with the landscape around them in homegrown poetry, prose and painting. The *Bulletin*, Sydney's nationalistic newspaper, sponsored a school of writing in which the ideal of the bush and the bushman was treated as a national legend. Writers like Henry Lawson, Joseph Furphy and Steele Rudd produced short, sharp views of bush life and its hardships and rewards, which were generally to be found in the loyalty of mates. Others, like Barbara Boynton in her story *Squeaker's Mate*, pointed out that whilst the loyalty and rewards went to the men, the hardships fell all too often on the women. Many of the *Bulletin* writers were consciously anti-British. They feared the trap which the novelist Rosa Pread had fallen into: 'In those early days . . . it never struck me that my worthiest ambition might be to become a genuine Australian storyteller.'

European influences were more easily accepted in the visual arts, both in black-and-white drawing and in Impressionism, which seemed to be made for the landscapes of Australia. Painters like Tom Roberts, Frederick McCubbin and Arthur Streeton banded together to paint Australian subjects in real landscapes. Not unnaturally, they were criticized for it and, as Humphrey McQueen has pointed out, it was not until the 1930s that their works, and that of many writers of the time, received recognition as examples of real Australian art.

Sport, that enjoyment of relaxation which old Sam Marsden had so disapproved of, made rapid progress. A nation which put leisure above overtime was able to prove they were the *right stuff* on the sports field, though there were more spectators than participants. That typical delight in the other man's failure was beginning to show, as Manning Clark says 'because the one thing Australians do know is failure: they know the failure of being unable to impose their will on their vast continent. They know they're going to be beaten by drought, by flood, by fire, by the rise and fall in world prices over which they have no control.'

## W.M. Hughes
The political parties had sorted themselves into two camps by 1910 and Labor and Liberal faced one another across the Federal Parliament. Labor, under Fisher, was in office from 1910 to 1913, with a brief

Liberal ministry under Cook. When war was declared, Labor won again, under W.M. Hughes, the most outstanding, and possibly the most devious political figure of the first quarter of the century.

Born in Wales, he arrived in Queensland in 1882 at the age of 22. He tried a number of jobs, including that of stone-breaker, before opting for a career in politics. His flamboyant manner in parliament made him as many enemies as friends. Hughes saw himself as a leader in the Lloyd George mould and felt a strong bond with the old country. He pressed for an Australian army and tabled a number of requests for conscription to be introduced. After a visit by General Kitchener, who also pointed out the vulnerability of the country, a military college was established and compulsory military training introduced. A small navy was manned and maintained by Australia. It was not long before the infant forces received their baptism.

# 5.
# THE DREAMER WAKES

'Out on the sea they could see something moving. They pondered what it was . . . What are they, the Aboriginals thought, and others replied that they were agula, devils. So they quickly told their wives and children to run away and hide in the caves far from the seaside. Quickly they gathered up their children and dogs and went up to the caves and left the men to see what they really were.

Some yelled out "Kill the white agula, see if they have blood in them," and so it happened, that's how the war started. They fought against one another, they killed some white people, and the white people killed the Aboriginals too. The Aboriginals found out they were really humans too, but still they didn't win. Then the white people took their lands and the Dreaming times were forgotten. And so no more hunting for free food and the water they used to drink out of rivers and gullies and springs; today and tomorrow were finished.'

'I am assigned servant to Mr Danger. I was at his station on Myall Creek, as hut keeper, for five months, in June 1838. There were some native blacks there. I have said there were 20 but I am sure there was that number and upwards. While

Master was away some white men came on a Saturday evening, about 10 in number. They came on horseback, armed with muskets, swords and pistols. All were armed. I was at home when they came. I was sitting with Kilmiester, the stock-keeper. The blacks were all encamped for the night. They were not more than two yards from the huts. This was an hour and a half before sundown. There were plenty of women and children among them. The blacks, when they saw the men coming, ran into our hut. Russell had a rope which was round the horse's neck and he began to undo it while the blacks were in the hut. I asked them what they were going to do with the blacks. Russell said "We are going to take them over the back of the range to frighten them." Russell and some one or two went in and I heard the crying of the blacks for relief or assistance to me and Kilmiester. They were moaning the same as mother and children would cry. There were small things that could not walk, there were a good many small boys and girls.

The party then went away with the blacks. All the blacks were tied together, they were tied with their hands, they were fastened with one rope, it was a tether rope for horses. It was a very long rope. They brought out the whole except two that made their escape as the men were coming up; they were two little boys and they jumped into the creek. One black gin they left with me in the hut, they left her because she was good-looking. There was one old man named Daddy, the oldest of the lot; he was called Old Daddy, he was an old, big tall man. This Daddy and another old man named Josey, they never tied along with the rest; they were crying and did not want to go; they made no resistance.

Some of the children were not tied, others were; they followed the rest that were tied. The small

ones, two or three, were not able to walk, the
women carried them on their backs in opossum
skins. They were not in sight above a minute or so
after they went away. About a quarter of an hour
later I heard the report of two pistols, one after
the others. I did not hear anything else.'

Twenty-eight people died that day at Myall Creek.
The reason behind the massacre was given as cattle-
bothering. The year was 1838 and the only remarkable
thing about the story is that the 11 murderers were
brought to trial. They were acquitted, a verdict which
was highly popular, and the Chief Justice had to exert
all his authority to prevent the court audience from
cheering. 'The aristocracy of the colony, for once, joined
heart and hand with the prison population in
expressions of joy.' But the authorities were not
satisfied and a retrial was ordered. Seven of the
accused were found guilty and hanged for the crime.
The prosecution was led by the Attorney General of
New South Wales . . . and the seven were convicted on
the evidence of a white servant. The remaining four
went free because the only evidence against them was
from an Aborigine, whose word was unacceptable
because he was ignorant of the ordinances of religion.

Just before the trial the *Sydney Herald* had
published an editorial on the Aborigines and their
rights:

'This vast country was to them a common – they
bestowed no labour upon the land – their
ownership, their right, was nothing more than
that of the emu or kangaroo. They bestowed no
labour upon the land and that – and that only – it
is which gives a right of property to it. Where, we
ask, is the man endowed with even a modicum of
reasoning powers, who will assert that this great
continent was ever intended by the Creator to
remain an unproductive wilderness? The British

people took possession and they had a perfect right
to do so, under the Divine authority, by which a
man was commanded to go forth and people and
till the land. Herein we find the right of the
British crown, or more properly, the British
people.'

It is not such a large step from that to this:

'I remember my old grandmother saying, if you see
a man on a horse, you run away and hide because
they're coming round to grab kids. And we did
that for about two years and then we finally got
caught. And we were taken to the Lutheran
mission at Knibba. And that's where we were
brought up.

We were brought up the real hard German way.
They were tough. You worked from daylight to
dusk. We made bread, we milked cows, we looked
after kids, we did sewing, we did cleaning. I was
only a little girl of thirteen and they had a little
stool for kids, girls, and we stood on it to reach the
dough, to punch the dough to make bread.

My dad was working on a station and we'd
probably see him once in 12 months, and it was
not always that we were allowed to go. It was so
disheartening for our mum and us kids if they
came and saw us for the day, then you'd start to
fret again, "Why was I taken away?". It took us
years to find our brother. He was always told that
his people were dead. My mum and dad didn't
have a clue where he had gone to. I didn't know
how to speak to my brother. He was a total
stranger. We'd been parted so long. I reckon it
took me two years to sit and talk to my mum.

They didn't have time to show any affection –
we had to work. I suppose you'd call it like a
concentration camp.'

The words are those of an Aboriginal woman in her fifties remembering . . . a memory shared by thousands of her people. A young man recalls being taken from his parents in the 1960s and placed in a home in Sydney:

> 'It wasn't the conditions, it was just the way we were treated . . . like animals not as human beings. Kicked, hit about, belittled when people came to see how the black people were getting on. I don't know if my parents came to visit. I don't remember.
>
> They knew where they'd come from, some of them, but not all of them. They're still trying to trace their brothers and sisters, if any. A lot of people were taken away because they were fairer and they were adopted out by white families. They went through life thinking they were white.'

But how did it happen this way, where did it all begin?

## Aborigines and the early settlers

In 1770 Captain James Cook saw the first Australians as:

> '. . . far happier than we Europeans. They live in a tranquillity which is not disturbed by inequality of conditions. The earth and sea of their own accord furnish them with all things necessary for life. They have very little need for clothing and seem to set no value upon anything we give them, nor would they part with anything of their own for any article we could offer them. This, in my opinion, argues that they think themselves possessed with all the necessities of life, and that they have no superfluities.'

The founding of the first colony at Sydney Cove

turned the local Aborigines into British subjects. It was held that the land was *terra nulleus*, had no owners, and therefore no treaties or wars of conquest were necessary before the British settled in.

A lie, the first of many that were to ignore obvious facts, but in the beginning the locals seemed to get on reasonably well with the newcomers. Arthur Phillip was fascinated that the Aborigines showed no fear of the settlers, though there were moments of confusion. Lt Philip Gidley King found himself and his companions confronting a group of natives who 'wanted to know of what sex we were, as they took us for women, not having our beards grown.' King ordered one of the party to drop his breeches and clear the matter up, at which the Aboriginals gave a great shout of admiration.

Phillip had a less inconvenient advantage. One of the rituals of the coastal peoples involved the removal of the right upper front tooth, the same Phillip lacked, and this gave him standing in their eyes. They were quite ready to establish contact of a limited nature, accepting the whites as part of the natural scheme of things. David Collins, the Judge Advocate, wrote:

> 'During the first six weeks, we received only one visit, two men strolling into the camp and remaining in it for about an hour. They appeared to admire whatever they saw and after receiving a hatchet, took their leave, apparently well pleased with their reception. The fishing boats also frequently reported their having visited by many of these people when hauling the seine; at which labour they often assisted with cheerfulness and in return were rewarded with part of the fish taken.'

The British wanted very little of the 'Indians' at Sydney Cove, and the 'Indians' wanted very little of the British. But things soon began to change. If there was one thing about the whites that was totally new, it was the speed with which they moved. They were fast. They lived with an awareness of the future and the rewards it might bring which was every bit as acute as the Aborigine's understanding of the past and the continuity of the Dreaming.

## Aborigines and the land

The settlers needed land, so they took it. They saw the land as it would become, when the trees were grubbed out, the bush burned off. They saw great flocks of sheep stretching from horizon to horizon. They saw the sky dark with the dust of massive cattle herds, or hazy with the smoke from factory chimneys. They saw nothing they could not achieve and nothing to stop them.

The Aborigines never thought of themselves as owners of the land. The land owned them, they were bound to it by an intricate system of duty, belief and obligation they could no more reject than they could tear out their nervous systems. For them the Dreaming was the land. They had no objection to others using the ground since they, white or Aboriginal, had no spiritual ties to it. Only the original dwellers in each country could perform the essential duties, and leasing or lending the land could not harm it. But to be deprived, cut off from the land, was a different matter.

The Aborigines saw their spiritual nature as being one with the body (unlike Christians, whose spirit would be rewarded or punished after death, free of the flesh) and they suffered their moral lessons during life. At the end, in death, body and spirit returned to the earth where they waited to become a child once more in an unending process. So when the whites stole the land and banished the people, they stole the soul too. As the settlers pushed forward, so they drove the Aborigines before them, out of their own countries and into the countries of other groups where they were unwelcome. Dislocation, confusion and inter-tribal violence were only the obvious consequences; far more serious was the attack on the spirit of a people.

Some whites made treaties, like John Batman. In 1835 he secured by private treaty 600,000 acres near Melbourne. The document read:

> 'Know all persons, that we, three brothers, Jagajaga, Jagajaga, Jagajaga, being the principal chiefs of a certain native tribe called Dutigallar, being possessed of the tract of land hereinafter mentioned and in consideration (of about £200 worth of trade goods) . . . do give, grant and confirm to the said John Batman all that tract of country situate and being in the bay of Port Phillip. Signed, sealed and delivered in the presence of us, having been fully and properly interpreted and explained to the said chiefs.'

It was nonsense. There were no chiefs in Aboriginal society, and there was no one who could give away or sell the land. They might as well give away the air they breathed, and Batman and his party knew it. One of them wrote, 'There is no such thing as chieftainship, but this is a thing which must be kept to ourselves or else it may affect the Deed of Conveyancing.'

On the positive side, the trick showed that at least Batman assumed the Aborigines had land; most whites didn't even grant them that. They saw no social organization they could recognize and assumed – through ignorance or for convenience – that there was none; some went so far as to assert that the Aborigines had no language beyond basic grunts and that they could be scattered and killed at the whim of the settler. Resistance was only a matter of time.

## Pemulwuy

The first and perhaps greatest of Australian patriots was born near the end of the eighteenth century. He was in his thirties when the British arrived at Sydney Cove. His name was Pemulwuy, in the local language, Man of the Earth. At first he accepted the whites,

117

getting to know some of them, joining his countrymen Bennelong and Colby in exploring the new culture.

Peace didn't last and by 1790 he had begun a war against the British which was to last 12 years, a unique consistency of resistance. He recruited escaped English and Irish convicts and led them in attacks on the farms and settlements of the invaders. His main weapon was fire. He burnt crops, buildings, thousands of acres of scrub because, as oral tradition tells us, he was prepared to see the end of himself, of his people and even of the land rather than allow it to pass into the hands of despoilers. As Professor Eric Wilmot says:

'He took on the best that the British in New South Wales could throw at him in the form of the NSW Corps, and defeated them. And yet he came from a society that had no military tradition. He is described as a very strange figure – he was seen as a clever man involved in spiritual things. At one stage he was shot in the head in an attack on Parramatta. He was brought into Sydney in a coma and it was seen by all that he wasn't going to live. And yet so concerned was Governor Hunter by the situation that he had the man chained hand and foot and locked in a cell with a guard mounted. And yet within two days Pemulwuy had escaped. He was to many of the British a strange goblinlike figure who haunted the foreshore and for some reason the settlers were determined not only to defeat him but to obliterate the evidence of his existence and for the best part of 200 years they were successful.'

In other parts of the country and throughout the nineteenth century, the resistance was sporadic, though in Tasmania it was remarkably effective. The Aborigines drove sheep and settlers from the land until the whites initiated a policy of genocide and began killing Aborigines indiscriminately.

In London The Aboriginal Protection Society was founded and pious sentiments uttered: 'It might be presumed that the native inhabitants of any land have an incontrovertible right to their own soil; a plain and sacred right, however, which seems not to have been understood.'

## Reserves and resistance

In Australia the view was different. The immigrant with a family to feed and a fortune to make, the convict looking for someone worse off than himself, the squatter needing more acres for his sheep, would leave high-minded ideals to those with time and a private income. Their concerns were more pressing. They would try to be humane, to protect the Aborigines from the violence of colonization, not by controlling the colonizers but, as Governor Arthur of Tasmania said in the 1820s, by settling them 'in some remote quarter, which should be strictly preserved for them'. They would be supplied with food and clothing and protected from the stock-keepers on condition 'of their confining themselves to certain limits beyond which, if they pass, they should be made to understand they will cease to be protected'.

Under the guise of caring this meant that Aborigines were fair game once they were off the land reserved for them. The land was reserved without any reference to them and because it had no possible value for the whites . . . yet. In 1828, in New South Wales, all Aborigines, were ordered out of districts settled by whites. Naturally enough, they resented this. As subjects of the crown they were denied its protection, but if they resisted, as subjects of the crown they were guilty of rebellion, not war.

It is not so much the violence of colonization which takes the breath away as the sheer hypocrisy. But perhaps many felt justified in so dealing with a people 'universally allowed to be the lowest race of savages in the known world', and whose 'extermination would be a great benefit to the whole country'.

The nature of tribal life made it impossible for the Aborigines to mount a sustained countrywide resistance. Though tribes did occasionally fight together, especially in Queensland, there was no leader like the American Sitting Bull, who held his people together long enough to gain a significant military victory. There would be no Little Big Horn in Australia.

The Aborigine's battles were fought in a thousand lonely places across the continent and without the benefit of firearms. Skirmishes tended to develop around outlying or relatively undefended settlements; vicious little fights where mercy or quarter were seldom given and black and white women and children fell to spear and knife. But the progress of the whites was inexorable. They knew that all the land would be theirs in the end, by one means or another:

> 'The niggers had something really startling to keep them quiet. The rations contained about as much strychnine as anything else and not one of the mob escaped. More than a hundred were stretched out by this ruse.'

> 'I have heard men of culture and refinement, of the greatest humanity and kindness to their fellow whites, talk not only of the wholesale butchery but of the individual murder of natives exactly as they would talk of a day's sport, or of having to kill some troublesome animal.'

> 'I had a white person say to me yesterday, "I come from the Western District and you know, my father knew Aborigines and I'd like to go and meet some." And I said: "I don't think you'd better go, because from that particular place, after church, the men would go out in shooting parties to kill Aborigines. Your father hasn't told you about that,

but we know he was one who was involved. So I wouldn't go up there trying to be friendly because you might get a hostile reaction. Because the people who experienced all this are still living." You think of history as happening way back in 1788 but history is living in every Aborigine family in this country.'

This last quote comes from Eve Fesle Jnr, an Aborigine linguist in her thirties.

## Let them die out

The fighting was bloody, but it was something that both sides understood. The peace, the process of pacification, the assimilation which was often extinction, the kindness and condenscension, the re-education . . . these were the real tragedies in the hearts of the people.

Once Aborigines were moved to reservations, or had such areas created around them, with white protectors, they felt they had lost all right to run their affairs and decide things for themselves. The chief protector in such places was the legal guardian of every Aborigine and half-caste child, whether the child had parents or not, until the age of 21. They were seen as infants, incapable of self-control, self-knowledge, moral balance or foresight. For some the process of improvement began with the trouser, 'for no sooner does the gospel begin to operate on the mind of the heathen than it leads to the first step in civilization – the necessity of a decent covering. It next induces a settled way of life . . . and tends to produce industry'.

Eve Fesle Snr, mother of the linguist, knew all about an industrious life:

'We were taught to fourth grade, just enough educated to be labourers and domestic servants. We were pretty clever some of us, don't you worry, but we never had the chance. At 13 you were sent out to work somewhere. They sent me to a place in Woombai and they used to give me three shillings and sixpence a week. They used to send most to the settlement and give me sixpence, and I used to stand up on a box to do the washing. I used to have to wash these big heavy flannel nightshirts the men used to wear and my little arms used to ache. And she even had me climbing the ladders and doing the walls, cleaning the walls. I was 13 and I was a thin little kid [laughs], I don't think there were any fat kids at the mission anyway, we were all thin. And, the woman where I worked, she used to make me unpick her clothes. I used to save the cotton, then she'd get me to cut down her dress and I reused the cotton. It was nice food at first, then she used to give me less food. I used to go out and fill up with mangoes. And for years after I couldn't stand the smell of a mango.'

Not everyone was in favour of missions. 'I do not think there is any necessity why we should go out of our way to preserve the Aboriginal population. We have taken possession of this country and according to all laws, the Aboriginal population must disappear entirely.'

Many thought this way . . . best let them die out. Others opted for assimilation or exploitation. During an investigation in the 1940s on a cattle station owned by a multinational company, it was reported that girls as young as seven had been forced into prostitution so that Europeans could avoid the risk of venereal disease from older girls.

Confined to one place, when everything in their culture from bodily health to spiritual well-being depended on a nomadic life, it was no wonder that the Aboriginal population began to fall. Clothing sheltered germs and damp which the sun would have destroyed; poor diet encouraged disease and did not fight its effects; despair induced drunkenness and the breakdown of family life. Values which had stood like rocks for over 40,000 years were contemptuously swept away.

Throughout the nineteenth and twentieth centuries, laws were built around the Aborigine, protecting him, suffocating him. Everything was mooted but leaving him to follow his own way of life. Many of these laws were well intentioned, but protection leads to restriction of liberty. All too often the only protection the Aborigines needed was from those who wanted to protect them.

## The Freedom Rides

Charles Perkins was brought up in an Aboriginal boys' home in Adelaide, where even as a youngster he felt the one-sided nature of Australian life. Things came to a head when a friend was turned down by the Australian navy because he was Aboriginal.

In America freedom was in the air, the civil-rights movement was gathering momentum and the ripple was spreading across the Pacific. Perkins threw himself into Australia's infant Rights Movement and spent some time abroad. Back in Australia he started the Freedom Rides, hiring a bus and, together with white students from New South Wales University, travelling through some of the most racist towns in the country:

Back in Australia he started the Freedom Rides, hiring a bus and, together with white students from New South Wales University, travelling through some of the most racist towns in the country:

'We went out to demonstrate that there was a lot of racism in these country towns – deep, embedded, vicious hatred. When we got to the town of Walgett, the RSL (the Returned Servicemen's League), they were the real bastion of racism in this country at that time, we demonstrated in front of it, and it is really ironic because all these men went away to fight for justice and equality and they came back into their own country and did just the opposite. You see blacks weren't even allowed into the RSL. I went back in 1986, 17 years after the freedom ride, and they still barred me, just because I was that person who had caused all that trouble and because I was an Aborigine.'

Shortly after the Freedom Rides, black cattle drovers in the Northern Territories stopped working and demanded equal wages and land rights on sheep stations owned by the Vestey family. There was a long and bitter struggle between the local people, the Gurinjdi, and the national and international mining and farming interests.

## Legal Struggles

One of those deeply involved was the poet Kath Walker, who tried to get backing and support from the ACTU, the body which represents the Trades Unions of Australia:

'We asked them to recognize the strike and they said, "No we can't, they haven't asked our permission to have it." And I said "For God's sake they don't know the word strike." And it wasn't until the university students went up there that the trade union movement came behind us. There was a song, the Gurinjdi song . .

Poor bugger me
Gurinjdi
Long time sit down
This country.
Work for little bit
Flour and sugar and tea
From Lord Vestey
To Gurinjdi
Poor bugger me.

They really held out – you see they couldn't do
without the Aboriginal stockmen in those days,
because they were the greatest horsemen. So they
won it, when they got the knowledge how to fight
from the students, not the ACTU.'

Kath Walker became involved in the struggle to
remove articles 51 and 127 from the Australian
constitution. Article 51 excluded Aboriginals from the
scope of laws and measures passed by parliament and
127 excluded them from the national census.
Aboriginal activists saw both as barriers to their
participation in the political life of the nation and
campaigned for a national referendum to have them
written out.

Prime Minister Robert Menzies was not keen. He
had already been rebuffed when he wanted to outlaw
the Communist party. However, his successor, Holt,
was less obdurate:

'He said, "If you can get a yes from every
politician in the House of Representatives and in
the Senate, then I'll consider a referendum." So for
months we lobbied and when it finally went to the
House and the Senate they were unanimous that
there should be a referendum. And we were in
business. On 27th May 1967 the people voted 93
per cent in favour. The people who didn't vote were
the country people who hated our guts anyway!'

In 1972 Aborigines from all over the country set up a
Tent Embassy on the lawns of Parliament House,
Canberra. They had their own flag: red for the land,
black for the people, and yellow for the sun and the
life-giving force which joins the people to the land.
Shortie O'Neill, an activist from Alice Springs,
remembers the feeling at the time:

'Those days we were all very proud to be
Aboriginal and we used to march and identify

ourselves. And many people who were Aboriginal and would not claim it the majority of those people are now Aboriginal because we've been able to turn it round and say Aboriginal is good . . . it's something to be proud of.'

## Land Rights and the future

No one involved in the Aboriginal movement believes that victory is in sight. There will be many years of struggle before real equality exists and whites realize that Aborigines can enrich society with a vision which is perhaps needed now more than ever.

Professor Eric Wilmot, one of the country's foremost Aboriginal thinkers says:

> 'Some Australians are moved by spiritual influences ranging from the Christian cross to the Rainbow Serpent; some are moved by passion, compassion . . . football matches and yacht races, but most aren't moved at all. We are the most sceptical people on earth and this can be a negative element because it makes it difficult for us to believe in a vision or a cause, even the great cause of the Aboriginal people. I don't think there is a cure for this but there might be an antidote and we must find it because our future is an experiment. But we are not simply the rats in the maze, we are also the judges and we will know how successful we are long before the rest of the world does.'

So far the results are in the balance. According to Eve Fesle Jnr:

> 'Home ownership for Aboriginal people is very low compared with other Australians – they live in low-cost rental. We have a lot of sickness among our people, which has an effect on school attendance. Children don't get enough to eat, they have hearing problems. Poor health, poor housing, no money, it sets up a poverty cycle. We need

money but we also need programmes set up by our own people because many Aborigines don't trust the whites and history shows we have no cause to.

We've all had to think about the future. About our need to have Land Rights; that we can set up the means to save our languages from extinction because they are dying at the rate of one a year. Soon we'll be running our own departments and making our own decisions. It'll be a long, long battle but we've survived 200 years. Our culture has changed, adapted itself, it hasn't died out and it's a tribute that one per cent of the population has achieved tremendous lobby power. I think we'll make it eventually – it won't be easy but it never had been easy since the Europeans first arrived on our shores.'

Land Rights, which advanced throughout the 1870s and early 1880s, have suffered from the economic recession. Mining becomes more important and more powerful, and the lure of the land is as strong as ever. Many fear that if economics once more dictate the course of human relationships, Aboriginal hopes will take a back seat, if they are even allowed on the bus.

Robert Brofoe, spokesman for the fringe dwellers of Western Australia, says, 'Instead of the government working out a solution to cope with the problems of mining, they plan for those things that are going to be profitable to the white people.'

And as for the bi-centenary . . .

'We don't see it as a joyous occasion – who could after the 200 years of oppression and denial of rights – it just means there is another 200 years of struggle to go.

We have to work hard to make our people the once proud people we were 200 years ago and not the degraded people we were 20 years ago. We've been around for 50,000 years and we'll never die out. The land doesn't belong to us, we belong to it.'

# 6.
# TOWARDS THE PACIFIC

In August 1914 a young Serbian nationalist assassinated Archduke Franz Ferdinand of Austria in Sarajevo. This led to the outbreak of the First World War.

Australian sentiment was, on the whole, behind Great Britain. Fisher, the leader of the Labor opposition, declared that Australia would support the mother country to the last man and the last shilling. Archbishop Kelly put the Catholic point of view: 'War is worse than pestilence, worse than famine. Yet war evokes patriotism, courage, fraternal regard . . . We should stand shoulder to shoulder with our responsible rulers and leaders.'

Patriotic songs were written, there were fund-raising events and young men volunteered (there was no conscription) in their thousands. For some the war was an answer to the material ease they saw as destroying the toughness of the nation. Others felt they would be redeemed; Henry Lawson, 'that great, marvellous drunkard', as Manning Clark calls him, 'thought that the war would clean his dirty slate'. It was a chance for adventure, and to see the rest of the world. It could also clear up an annoyance closer to home.

Australian troops landed in German New Guinea in September 1914. They mopped up German resistance and took over the territory, to general rejoicing at home. Another success followed. The German raider

*Emden* had been causing considerable trouble to shipping in the Pacific. When she was tracked down and destroyed, a ship of the Australian navy, the cruiser *Sydney*, was part of the task force.

The young continued to flock to the training camps where they were weighed, re-clothed and warned about the diseases which lay in wait for soldiers. They were handed over to the corporals and sergeants from England for parade-ground training. The experiment wasn't a success. Men from the bush had no respect for a uniform and a loud mouth; black-eyed and prone NCOs became a common sight on parade. It was a characteristic of Australian troops throughout the war. They refused to put up with the petty regulations and pointless discipline which bedevilled the British army, and they proved, to the annoyance of many English officers, that such regulations had nothing to do with making courageous and effective fighting men.

## Gallipoli

The war soon became bogged down. After the disasterous Russian defeat at Tannenburg at the close of 1914, Britain and France were locked with Germany in the mud of Flanders. Movement would have to be elsewhere.

The Allied War Council decided in January 1915 to launch a naval expedition against the Gallipoli peninsula in the north of Turkey. The military operation would be a combined British-Australian effort and troops gathered in Egypt to train and await embarkation. Egypt was not to the taste of the Australians, who described it as 'the land of sin, sun, sand, shit and syphilis'. By April 1915 they were anxious for action.

The Anzacs (Australian and New Zealand Army Corps) were landed at Gaba Tepe on the western shore of Gallipoli on the night of 25th April. The ocean was calm and there was a bright half moon. Searchlights played over the troops as they headed for shore in long lines of boats, snaking towards the deserted beach. The men were quiet and confident, but the British had directed the flotilla to the wrong cove. They were almost at the beach when they were spotted by Turkish defences and firing began. Wading waist high through the water, they fought their way ashore where they found steep cliffs instead of the flat sand they had been promised. They stormed these and fought their way to the top, where they faced troops under the command of Mustafa Kemal (later President and the founder of modern Turkey). He stopped the advance, but could not dislodge the Anzacs from their hard-won ground.

The British commanders favoured withdrawal. They did not believe the Anzacs could hold on, but they did, day after day, night after night, digging into the stony soil and resisting each new attack. For months they endured the heat of a Turkish summer and flies more avid than those at home.

Neither army moved, but both kept up such a constant fire, that not a finger could be raised above the parapet without risk. The Anzacs invented the periscope rifle which could be aimed and fired from cover. The Turks lobbed grenades and mortar-bombs. Another fighting front had ground to a halt, though as autumn approached the situation became more lethal.

In August, at the battle for Lone Pine, the Australians lost 2,000 men and won seven Victoria Crosses. A rash of vicious little actions broke out, with heavy casualties for minimal gains. The men remained cheerful as winter arrived with freezing rain, howling winds and night-time temperatures so low that ill-clad guards froze to death. They also managed a smile through gritted teeth when the general withdrawal of Allied forces was announced.

They did not consider they had been defeated; it was a loss in the tradition of a hard-fought game. Many in Australia saw the episode in the same way they regarded sport – showing that the country still had more than enough of the right stuff:

'To one thing Australians may look forward with confident pride. The men who at Anzac (the landing beach had been re-named in honour of the Australian-New Zealand forces) and Suvla Bay performed prodigies of valour will acquit themselves not less valiantly wherever the future of war may henceforth take them.'

On the first anniversary of the Gallipoli landings a day of remembrance was announced and a new myth was born or perhaps created:

'Anzac Day, which we have celebrated for the first time, and celebrated, we hope, in a solemn and thoughtful mood, means more than an immortal charge up the cliffs of Gallipoli . . . It reminds us of the day Australians really knew themselves. Australia is now no longer a prosperous country in which it is good to live – the blood of our dead heroes was shed afar from us, but their spirit has come home across the seas . . . to whisper that we have taken our place among the nations.'

## Australian-British or Australian-Australian

This reverence for the courage and suffering at Gallipoli would remain, but unthinking support for the British war effort was beginning to waver. The heroism of Lone Pine was to become the hell of the Western Front where casualties mounted at a dizzying rate.

At Pozières Ridge in France, over 23,000 Australians were lost in a six-week period. For what? In Moree and Kalgoorlie, Benella and Julia Creek they were asking whether they wanted to buy a piece of France with Australian blood. But every day more men were needed for the nation to maintain her commitment, as Prime Minister William Morris Hughes was determined she should. He said that to fight with anything less than total effort would be to commit national suicide by slowly bleeding to death. The only answer lay in overwhelming Germany by force of numbers, and for that Australia would need to introduce conscription.

On the surface this was an innocent enough proposal, in line with Allied policy in Europe. However, Hughes encountered a tidal wave of feeling in the country which divided everyone into Australian-British or Australian-Australian. These divisions had always been present. They went back to the struggle of the New South Wales Corps to import goods against the wishes of the settlers who wanted to make something out of the country. The conscription crisis gave people two defined parties and a choice where they were going to nail their colours.

Hughes set out with characteristic energy to convince the nation. He travelled through all the states, speaking at crowded meetings, undaunted by rotten eggs in Queensland. The tide was against him, however, particularly when news of the Irish Easter rebellion of 1916 reached Australia. The brutality in putting down what many regarded as a genuine popular uprising did not endear the British to the Australian public. They saw no reason why the descendants of Irish Catholics should put themselves in the front line and release another English soldier to harass the people of Ireland. Archbishop Mannix became their spokesman:

> 'The historian Edmund Campion describes Mannix as a tall, piercing-eyed ecclesiastic who could command a crowd with his wit and with his irony. He was always on stage, always aware that people were looking at him and was, for that reason, a good community leader. He was the voice of that Australia which was striving to be born, free of the trammels of the British Empire.'

Hughes, a tiny wizened man with the complexion of a lizard, was also a powerful public speaker, a man who saw politics as a contest in which the weak would go to the wall. He was, however, in a difficult position as leader of a Labor Party with a large Irish Catholic anti-conscription wing. Most of his support came from his political opponents, the Protestant Empire Loyalists of the Liberal Party, but Hughes was no coward. He formed an alliance with the Loyalists and, turning the issue into a sectarian one, directed his fire at the Archbishop.

Conscriptionist newspapers highlighed Mannix's speeches and ignored or downgraded the pronouncements of other anti-conscriptionist leaders. Irish maids were sacked from Government House and vigilante committees were set up to exclude Catholics or working-class unionists from public office.

There was, however, one issue upon which both sides were agreed: the threat of Japanese expansion through the Pacific, which would be immeasurably aided by the collapse of Britain and the Empire. The conscriptionists felt that troops in France would lessen Japanese influence on their British allies; the 'antis' believed that Australian troops should police their own part of the globe.

Hughes called a referendum which came down firmly against conscription. This put him in a tricky position, with many in his own party unable to back him. The solution was a split and, taking a Labor rump, Hughes agreed a coalition with the Liberal party and formed a national government. Labor never forgave him; in their eyes he was a class traitor and a betrayer of socialist ideals.

### Heroic feats
By 1918 Australian forces had won a reputation as tough and dangerous fighters who were thrown into battle again and again where opposition and conditions were toughest. Their commander, General John Monash, the son of a Polish Jew, was a civil engineer who had indulged his interest in warfare as a part-time soldier in Victoria. Once war began, his rise was rapid.

He believed in pre-planning and the care of his troops to a degree unequalled until Montgomery in the Second World War. Lloyd George said he was the most able general on the Allied side, others that he was the best Jewish general since Joshua. It was strongly rumoured that had not the war ended when it did, he might have become Commander-in-Chief.

In August 1918 Monash and his troops took a supposedly impregnable German position at Mont St Quentin in what Liddell Hart called the finest feat of the war. It was a true national effort because men from all the states took part. The attack relied for its success on small groups acting on their own initiative but as part of a larger scheme. These same troops had been instrumental in holding up the final German offensive of March 1918. The fighting had been hard, the losses high and many in the front line felt they had been betrayed by Australian communists back home. They reasoned that the Australian party's recognition and support for the Bolshevik Revolution had aided the Russian withdrawal from the war and allowed the enemy to mount their last-ditch attack. This mood was to have considerable effect after the war when returned Anzacs were less inclined towards radical politics than their brothers-in-arms in Europe.

## Disillusion with Britain

It has been said often enough that after the First World War the old world was never the same again. For Australians too, attitudes were changing.

Britain had always been a distant and mysterious homeland, the source, the fount from which all blessings flowed. But now Australians were seeing the realities of British life and policy at close hand and they were not always impressed. A letter quoted in Bill Gammage's record of the war, *The Broken Years*, shows a fairly typical Anzac response to field punishments:

'There was a Tommy in the lines of the next camp

tied to a wooden cross. Everyone crowded round and started asking questions. It transpired that the poor devil had abused a lance-corporal and had to do two hours morning and afternoon for his trouble. Someone suggested cutting him free. The suggestion was no sooner made than carried out. The poor beggar kept saying, "Don't cut me free, chum, I'll only get more." The raiders assured him he would not get any more while they were around. Having destroyed the cross, pelted the officers' huts with bricks and jam tins and named them for a lot of Prussian bastards, the raiders returned to our lines.'

On the whole, rank meant very little to the Australians. A uniform, an expensive education and the right accent gained derision rather than respect. That had to be earned on the battlefield.

Many other aspects of British life caused surprise, particularly to those who had been on leave in England. They found a cold, poky, class-ridden society which had nothing to do with the fabled heart of the Empire. Many wondered why the English didn't give the place to the Kaiser and move somewhere warmer. The people, labouring for endless hours in their factories, seemed smaller, and this might have been true. Good diet and a healthy climate had produced a startling change in the children and grandchildren of immigrants. Compton Mackenzie wrote of the Anzac troops at Gallipoli:

'There was not one of these glorious young men I saw that day who might not himself have been Ajax, Hector or Achilles. Their almost complete nudity, their tallness and majestic simplicity of line, their rose-brown flesh burnt by the sun and purged of all grossness by the ordeal through which they were passing, all these united to create something as near to absolute beauty as I shall ever hope to see in this world.'

## General disillusion

Back in Australia the nation went about its business.
Among farmers there was more concern about the
drought and a plague of rabbits than about the war.
The Newcastle steel works was opened, income tax
introduced and the marketing of wheat organized,
which helped the farmers to recover from drought and
rabbits alike. There was, however, concern among the
families of fighting men; Australia had sent a higher
proportion of its population to the war than any other
nation and was to suffer proportionately higher
casualties.

The Armistice saw the return of the Anzacs to a
future no more certain in Australia than it was in
Europe. The predominant mood of the post-war years
was disillusion. Manning Clark says the experience:

'. . . speeded up the decline of religious faith in
Australia. The effect was to raise the question in
the minds of Australians, could there possibly be a
benevolent creator of the universe or, as the editor
of a socialist paper put it in 1919: "Father, what
did you do during the World War?" It wasn't just
the undermining of religious faith, it was also an
undermining of secular, humanist faith, or the
faith in the enlightenment of Australia.'

## The Peace Conference

Prime Minister Hughes had no uncertainties when he
attended the Versailles Peace Conference. He intended
to safeguard the White Australia policy, ensure the
future of New Guinea and thwart the Japanese. His
chance to do the latter came when Japan tabled a
motion which would bind all members of the League of
Nations to 'accord to all alien nationals equal and just
treatment in every respect, either in law or in fact'.

Hughes exerted his influence and the motion was
rejected. The Japanese tried again, calling for an
endorsement of the principle of the equality of nations

and the just treatment of their nationals. This was carried, but not unanimously and the chairman, America's President Wilson, declared it lost. For Hughes, this was the greatest thing the Australian delegation achieved.

On German New Guinea, which Australia had invaded in the early years of the war, Hughes said, 'While no other nation would be threatened by Australia's possession of the islands, the acquisition of the place by another nation would constitute a menace to Australia. As Ireland is to the United Kingdom, as Mexico is to the United States . . . so is New Guinea to Australia.'

It was a far-fetched parallel and one which President Wilson did not accept. After much wrangling, a special C-class mandate was arrived at, which was a virtual annexation by Australia of New Guinea and other German territories. Australia did not have to grant equal trading rights to other nations, principally to the Japanese. President Wilson fought against these measures, but could not prevail against Hughes. On one occasion, wishing perhaps to belittle Australia's position, Wilson asked, 'How many do you speak for, Mr Prime Minister?' Hughes came back, 'For sixty thousand dead, Mr President'. There was no answer to that.

Australia regarded America with suspicion and was determined to watch her expansion into Asia and the Pacific. America regarded Australia as a small part of the British Empire. Despite the lessons of the war, this was how many Australians still saw themselves.


## THE TWENTIES AND THIRTIES

'More British than the British', was an attitude, some might have said a curse, which still lay heavily on Australia. Many of the returned men found, after the first heady days, a situation in which job prospects fluctuated rapidly.

Change was in the air; there were moves to create a centralized union; the Communist Party took wing, offering a new home to many of Labor's keenest minds, who were still suffering from the split caused by the conscription issue. The returned soldiers, despite their experiences, did not turn to the party; revolutionaries were no friends of theirs. Cries urging white Australia to 'wake up, turn red and follow the example of your despised yellow brothers', fell on deaf ears. When the Returned Service Leagues were formed to aid ex-servicemen, conservatives of all ranks and classes flocked to their standards. There were monster meetings at which extremists were attacked and broad hints dropped that the returned soldiers would not forever tolerate a country open to radicals.

The swing towards conservative values led to the formation of the Country Party, composed of farming and wool-growing interests, who felt that the wealth they were creating wasn't reflected in their political clout. By 1922 they had 10 seats in Parliament and, under their leader, Earle Christmas Grafton Page, formed a coalition with W.M. Hughes's National Party. Hughes's lifelong policy of central planning, however, was anathema to the Country Party and he had to step down as leader. He was to get his own back in characteristic fashion some years later when he was given a dinner to celebrate his 50 years in Parliament. The leader of the Country Party said that in his long career Billy Hughes had belonged to every political party except the Country. Hughes replied that he'd had to draw the bloody line somewhere.

**Men, money and markets**
The new government was headed by Stanley Bruce, an Australian-Briton who spoke with an English accent, wore tailored English clothes and had been educated at Cambridge rather than Melbourne University.

His policy came to be known as 'men, money and markets', and was tied directly to Britain. She would supply migrants and massive loans from the City to build up Australia's primary produce: wool, dairy products and fruit, which would be sold back to Britain. From Australia's point of view, there were a few snags. Manning Clark points out that she was to remain persistently materially backward in comparison with Western Europe. That she would agree to take British manufactured goods and not push for the development of Australian industry. That she would take Britain's surplus population as migrants who would be in competition with Australians for jobs and to become farmers. These problems weren't immediately obvious and the new government swept on through the 1920s, creating a tide of prosperity.

Not all, of course, was peaceful. The Labor movement, though bereft of central leadership, had been active in industrial affairs and Melbourne criminals had enjoyed a police strike in 1923. Police forces switched to motor transport, a new trend everywhere. American, British and Australian firms were producing vehicles for a market which, by the end of the decade, had bought 650,000 lorries, cars and bicycles. Electricity ran the city railways and some homes. Work was started on the Sydney Harbour bridge, and parents complained of their 'uncontrolled daughters' who had to be 'in the swim and sophisticated as they smoked and downed cocktails.'

The Federal Parliament Building in the nation's new capital city, Canberra, opened in 1927, in the presence of the Duke and Duchess of York. The city had been founded in 1913. In 1924 Bruce held an open air cabinet meeting there, surrounded by flies. He was ridiculed for it, but his time came when, 'looking like a man who carried a wax impression of St Peter's key in his pocket', he officiated at a ceremony where Melba sang and fruit punch was served, and where a lone Aborigine watched bemused while 400 hand-picked officials applauded politely. If they had listened hard, they might have heard the white ants gnawing at the nation's floorboards and realized that the bottom was about to drop out of the boom.

## The Great Depression

The West was slipping into an economic decline. Australia, as a primary producer, felt the effects sooner than most. Under the men, money and markets policy she had received vast loans from Britain. Now, with the downturn, she found her trade balance totally upset; England was no longer interested in buying her produce. Worse, she was in grave danger of being unable to service her debts. An economist, Otto Niemeyer, arrived from the Bank of England and summed up the situation:

> 'In recent years Australian standards have been pushed too high relative to Australian productivity and to general world conditions and tendencies. Australia has to adjust herself to a world economic situation more disadvantageous to herself than in the last decade. Australia is off budget equilibrium, off exchange equilibrium and faced by considerable unfunded and maturing debts both externally and internally.'

There was no chance of further borrowing to service those loans. Niemeyer recommended drastic deflation because higher repayments would soon be due. Australia must, he said, get her house in order by then, if only, as many Australians thought, to make sure that London markets didn't suffer from her default.

There was a feeling that perhaps Australia should begin to put herself first, rather than be continually subservient to a Britain which assumed it could still call the tune. But, as Humphrey McQueen says, there was no Lenin in Australia. There was only Jack Lang, the red Premier of New South Wales, who advocated a policy of ignoring the national debt in favour of financing socialist measures at home. With the slogan 'Lang is greater than Lenin', the Premier provoked hostility and support about equally and was in the end sacked for a breach of federal law.

Faced with the slump, Prime Minister Bruce had no freedom of action. Near the end of his ministry he began to feel suspicious of British motives, but he could not escape the fact that the nation was, as Niemeyer said, living on borrowed time. There had to be a lowering of the standard of living to ward off the day of reckoning.

The country was in no mood for this kind of talk. Everywhere businesses were crashing, farms and shops were closing, and an army of jobless was filling the roads of the nation. Attacked by Labor as a tool of the rich, Bruce was defeated on a bill to de-federalize industrial relations on the docks. The vote had been engineered by Billy Hughes, who expected to be asked back into the Labor government which emerged victorious from the subsequent elections. There is a story that he walked up and down in front of the Labor Party room in Parliament House, expecting to be invited in. He was not; the Labor Party never forgave Hughes. In his disappointment, he had the comfort of knowing that the Labor leader, Scullin, with a majority in only the lower House, was a prisoner of the economic situation. Huge strikes spread through the mining industry over an intended wage-cut of 12 per cent. Confrontations between strikers and authority resulted in a young miner being shot dead.

## Cricket and radio

Spirits were raised when Amy Johnson arrived by air and the King of England via the talkies. The Labor government departed and was replaced by a United Australia-Country Party coalition, but there was no relief for the unemployed. Thousands of families drifted into shanty towns around the cities. Sydney's was known, with wry humour, as Happy Valley. Others tramped the road or formed themselves into left- or right-wing associations out of sheer desperation and the need to do something.

A member of one, the New Guard, disrupted the opening of the Sydney Harbour bridge by charging into the assembled dignities on a shaggy horse and cutting the ribbon with his sword. The man, De Groot, received congratulatory telegrams from all over the nation, and said he felt that the bridge, as a symbol of power, should be opened by an ordinary Australian rather than by red Premier Jack Lang. But Australians are not inclined to join extremist parties and the New Guard and its like withered away.

A bigger shock to the nation was the death of idolized racehorse, Phar Lap, in 1932. The newspaper sellers' placards said only: 'He's Dead'. No name was needed to identify the nation's favourite. He was flown home, stuffed and put in a glass case in the National Museum. His heart, twice normal size, went on display at the Institute of Anatomy in Canberra and attracted reverent crowds.

A year later many Australians were to wish they could stuff English cricketer Douglas Jardine and put him in a glass case. A Briton, born in India like Sturt before him, he suffered from the English class system and was determined to prove himself. He became a caricature of the arrogant Pom (a word which had been in use since before the First war.) To overcome the genius of Don Bradman, the English masterminded a bowling attack intended to render stroke play impossible and send Bradman scurrying for cover. National fury erupted over this as much as over the cricket which was, in present day terms, gentle enough.

Perhaps some of the anger was aroused by the immediacy of the events reported live on the new radio service. The Australian Broadcasting Commission had been created from a countrywide network of class-A stations which had been existing on minimal licence fees. A second net of stations, class-B, which had received no official funding, went on to become commercial broadcasters, relying on advertising for their revenue. This growth of radio provided a cultural shock, introducing much of the country to great music and drama, on-air religion, sport, soap opera, Winnie Wattle, quiz shows and popular music.

The last years of the 1930s saw a gradual upturn in the economy. Wool exports found a new customer in the old enemy, Japan, which needed to clothe and supply an army busy conquering China. Opinion on whether it was wise to sup with this particular devil was, as usual, divided. It was quite possible the Japanese might use the spoils of their victory to finance and supply an invasion of Australia.

Workers at Port Kembla, the second largest iron and steel plant in the country, agreed. Even though jobs were still so scarce that the unemployed queued outside Kembla, known as 'The Blood House', waiting to fill the place of a dead or injured man, they drew the line at sending pig-iron to Japan to use against China. Robert Menzies, the new leader of the National Government, wasn't able to persuade them to return to work, but the government side-stepped the issue by pretending they'd run out of ore. Menzies earned the nickname of Pig-Iron Bob.

**Robert Menzies**

Menzies was 44 in 1938. The son of a politician, he had studied for the Bar, and was elected to the Victorian State Legislature in the 1920s and to the Federal Parliament in 1934. He was spotted by Joseph Lyon, leader of the Coalition, and appointed Attorney General. Lyon died in 1938 and, after a brief period, Menzies became Prime Minister.

He was a man of wit, a popular speaker who could sum up an argument in a few pithy sentences. In a sense, he was a tragic character who had been bowled over on a visit to London in 1934 by a vision of Britain as a sort of secular heaven. According to Manning Clark, Menzies came to the conclusion that the British class system was the most effective guarantee against communist revolution in Australia. Up to a point his adulation of the British sprang from this conviction.

Certainly Menzies was an Australian-Briton from top to toe at that stage. As the situation in Europe seemed to be moving once more towards war, he did not doubt that if the mother country fought, Australia would be there.

This was something of a side-issue for many. Their fears were directed towards a country which was, so far, reserving its wrath for the Chinese. Japan was biding her time, trying to find the raw materials, the oil and the rubber which trade embargoes were denying her. Australian concern was directed to the east while Britain concentrated on Europe and, almost incidentally, managed Australian foreign policy. Australia was reluctant to assume full Dominion status within the British Empire. There was concern that once this happened a Governor could no longer sack a state premier, as in the Lang case, and that the organic unity between the two nations would be lost. Dominion status was not accepted until 1941, when the nation was deeply involved in the Second World War.

The 1930s ended in Victoria with devastating bush fires. After a long drought, a number of fires started across the state, obliterating millions of acres and many small towns. Precautions were hopelessly inadequate; nothing men could do made the slightest difference. On Friday 13th January 1939, when many of the smaller fires began to combine, 'it appeared that the whole state was alight. Steel girders and machinery were twisted by heat as if they had been made of fine wire. Balls of crackling fire sped at great pace in advance of the fires, consuming, with a roaring, explosive noise, all that they touched . . . Such was the force of the wind that in many places hundreds of trees of great size were blown clear of the earth, tons of soil with embedded masses of rocks still adhering to the roots.'

It was Black Friday. The land reminded the people of its awesome power and of their impotence.

## THE SECOND WORLD WAR

'Fellow Australians. It is my melancholy duty to inform you officially that, in consequence of the persistence of Germany in her invasion of Poland, Great Britain has declared war upon her, and that, as a consequence, Australia is also at war.'

Australia had a conscript army which could not be sent abroad to fight and was known as the Koalas, after the marsupial of that name, which was protected from hunting and export. As in the First war, the call went out for volunteers. The pay was six shillings a day and for many it was the answer to long-term unemployment. They were known as the six-bob-a-day men and trained, as did their predecessors, in Egypt. They were considered wild, hard to control but remarkably effective in the line.

The first, phoney months of the war passed. Prime Minister Menzies sat in on the deliberations of the British war cabinet and agreed to an Australian presence in Egypt. In the early months of 1940 Tobruk was captured, and two Anzac divisions marched into Benghazi. Two further divisions (with the New Zealand division) were sent to Greece to stiffen the resistance of the national forces to the German advance. They were unable to do this and were driven back to Crete where they suffered airbone attack and defeat; 1,600 were killed and over 5,000 captured. Australian opinion of British strategy plummeted and spirits were not improved by German advances in the desert, under their commander Rommel.

Menzies faced mounting criticism from the country

and the parliamentary opposition, who refused to join a national coalition. Labor simply didn't believe that he was the man to lead a war effort independent of the United Kingdom. Australia had opened a legation in Tokyo in 1940, but there were few who did not feel a profound suspicion of Japanese Imperial ambitions. Even fewer considered that Menzies was the leader to face that threat. He had to go, and he did, handing over the direction of the war to the Labor leader, John Curtin.

### John Curtin

A forthright and competent man, Curtin had left school at the age of 13 and worked his political passage through the union movement. During the First war he had been a prominent opponent of conscription. After it he had, for a time, been an equally prominent drinker, a trait which sometimes seems *de rigueur* in the apprenticeship of Labor leaders. He educated himself in economic theory and, though he was said to be weak in international affairs, he had no doubt of the country's place at the centre of things rather than on the edge of Empire.

He became leader of his party in 1937 and found a large membership of Irish Catholics supportive of Franco and Mussolini. They tended towards a policy of appeasement of the dictators of Europe. A passionate anti-fascist, Curtin concentrated on regaining the support of the voters and rebuilding unity within a party shattered by its experience of the slump. Only in 1941, when he had office thrust upon him, was he able to pursue a more vigorous course.

New alliances had to be forged with the great Pacific power of the United States. In July 1941 Curtin made this shift in policy plain to Prime Minister Winston Churchill, when he asked that two Anzac divisions defending Tobruk against Rommel should be withdrawn and placed under direct Australian control. Churchill was not pleased, but 'if you insist, I shall agree'. Curtin insisted. The troops were withdrawn, though not before their resistance had broken the spirit of the Germans. The siege of Tobruk was lifted shortly after they left, but went almost unnoticed. In Hawaii, at the American base of Pearl Harbor, Australian nightmares had become real.

## Singapore falls and Darwin is bombed

Two days later Curtin declared war on Japan, independently of Britain. He was staking a claim in the Pacific and rammed the message home in his New Year address to the nation:

> 'The Australian government regards the Pacific struggle as primarily one in which the United States and Australia must have the fullest say in the direction of the democracies' fighting plan.
>
> Without any inhibitions of any kind, I make it quite clear that Australia looks to America, free of any pangs as to our traditional links or kinship with the United Kingdom.
>
> We know the problems the United Kingdom faces. We know the constant threat of invasion. We know the danger of dispersal of strength, but we know, too, that Australia can go and Britain can still hold on.
>
> We are, therefore, determined that Australia shall not go, and we shall exert all our energies towards the shaping of a plan, with the United States as its keystone, which will give our country some confidence of being able to hold out until the tide of battle swings against the enemy.'

The swing was firmly against the Allies. The Japanese armies advanced remorselessly through Malaya, hardly pausing before snapping up the ill-defended fortress of Singapore, where they captured 17,000 Australians among other Allied forces. Two of Britain's greatest battleships, the *Prince of Wales* and the *Repulse*, were sunk by Japanese planes off the coast of Malaysia.

It was a hammer blow to the idea that Britain could still defend a far-flung Empire and, as Geoffrey Blainey says, more than any other event since Federation, prompted Australia's search for other allies. This was marked once again by self-determination in the movement of Anzac troops. Two divisions from the desert war were being sent to Java and Sumatra, but Singapore had fallen during their transit. Curtin, facing the collapse of Empire defences and the threat of Japanese invasion, asked for their immediate return to Australia. Churchill was shocked that his judgement and leadership were being questioned. Curtin held his ground, and, in due course the troops were returned.

They were, no doubt, a comfort as the Japanese threat grew. In February 1942, Japan bombed Darwin. A warning was phoned in from a spotting post by a missionary priest, but the defences were woeful and the Japanese bombed virtually unopposed. Some American fighters were refuelling on the airstrip and, though five were destroyed on the ground, five were able to strike back and salve wounded pride. There was chaos on the ground; 300 died, 400 were wounded. A mass exodus was organized and there was an unofficial rush by a few, including a Chinese who intended to ride his three-wheeled ice-cream cart the 3,000 miles to Melbourne. There were over 100 bombing raids along the north coast. The government, with an excess of caution, imposed strict censorship and few were made public. Even the Darwin raid, which could hardly be kept a secret, was played down and the casualty list given as 17.

## The Americans arrive

'Early in 1942, I must have been 12, my parents took us all down to the seaside for a holiday – just at the entrance of Melbourne's harbour. We were sitting on the beach one day and in came a line of troop ships and you could see the white faces, about two miles away, lining the decks of those ships. We learned later that these were the first American troops coming into our part of Australia and my mother still talks of the intense emotional satisfaction that someone was coming to Australia's aid at what was the bleakest part of the war.'

The arrival of General Douglas MacArthur was akin to a second coming for many, as long as the black Americans kept decently clear of the cities. The country, which had just got over a mini-submarine attack on Sydney harbour, was reassured. Curtin got on well with the flamboyant MacArthur. To MacArthur, Australia was an aircraft carrier, a staging depot where America would build up the forces necessary to retake the Pacific. By the end of 1942, the battles of the Coral Sea and Midway had destroyed Japanese naval power. The tide had turned.

In the desert the Germans had been held near Alexandria. The Allies began to push them back, first at El Alamein and then to Tunis. The Afrika Korps surrendered. Australian troops were transferred from the desert to New Guinea, where the contest was to be long and bitterly fought.

## New Guinea
The Japanese invaded New Guinea in March 1942, landing at Gona and Buna in the north, where they overcame the resistance of local militia, farmers and missionaries, and advanced across the country, heading for Port Moresby.

They had to cross the Owen-Stanley Mountains, a barrier of 13,000 feet, pitted with passes and valleys, floored with almost impassable undergrowth, criss-crossed by rivers and drenched daily by monsoon rains. The Japanese objective was to use Port Moresby as a jumping-off point for the invasion of Australia.

Australia had a small force in New Guinea, and a few slow fighter planes. These were no match for the Japanese and the Anzacs were driven along the Kokoda trail, a narrow, winding path, often with room for no more than one man. They held steady for a while at the village of Kokoda, but were outnumbered and forced back towards the sea. The Japanese pushed forward, extending their supply lines, certain that they would carry out their objective with speed. But Australian reinforcements were now arriving, and in August 1942 the retreat stopped and held for four days at Isurava. The Japanese threw in everything they had. One Australian platoon repulsed 11 attacks, and an Australian corporal killed 40 Japanese and extricated his comrades from danger.

Over the following weeks, Australians fought and withdrew, wearing down the Japanese morale and extending their supply lines. Like the Australians, the enemy depended on the native population for everything which had to be carried, from tins of bully beef to wounded men. The people of New Guinea were treated by both sides as beasts of burden: men were forced from their villages to perform the tasks required of them. If they refused, they were beaten and threatened that their children would be sent to work in their stead. They got perhaps a handful of rice a day and, after the war, a few pounds for two years of back-breaking work. They played an important part in the eventual freeing of their island from an invader whom, on the whole, they rather preferred to the whites.

### Jungle fighting

War is never fair, and the Australian troops were enduring conditions among the worst in the world. On the jungle trails, peering through the dense foliage, occasionally blinded by shafts of sun, sinking waist deep into swamp, bitten and scoured by insects, each man fought a lonely battle.

Enemies would meet face to face, man to man on the trail. Snipers sat in trees and let half a patrol through before picking off an NCO or officer. Wounded men would crawl miles to avoid capture and certain death at the hands of the Japanese. The trail rose and fell thousands of feet in a few hundred yards. Engineers cut a hill path of 3,500 steps on the sheer slopes of the Maguli Range, and, as John Laffin points out, the torrential rain could turn that stairway into liquid mud in the course of an afternoon.

The intense damp heat by day and the freezing night-time temperatures caused great physical discomfort, destroying clothes, draining oils from the skin, turning hands into soggy paws and feet to pulp. Soldiers removing their socks would often peel away the soles of their feet, too. It was fighting which depended on the morale of each man and was seen, in the jungle and on the mainland that was so vulnerably close, as a battle of national importance. Humphrey McQueen says of it:

'Gallipoli is usually held as the moment when the Australian nation was born. If it was, it was a still-birth because it was divided and split over conscription and a whole range of political, religious and social issues. What happens in New Guinea, at Kokoda, is that a national focus is provided with Curtin as Prime Minister who leads a consensus and brings everything back into the fold of Australianness. Society is re-united. The war becomes the opportunity for people to believe that Australia is a place . . . worthy of effort and sacrifice.'

The Australians managed to manhandle two 25-pounder guns along the trail. They were the only artillery on either side. Firing 700 shells, which also had to be carried, they drove the Japanese back but victory was not to come without more hard fighting. The Japanese were starving, sometimes eating their own dead, but they fought on, seeing surrender as dishonour. But the end was inevitable. The Australians advanced 'forward on hands and knees, backwards on backsides', as they put it, and by January 1943 the enemy were driven out.

The Japanese were on the retreat everywhere during 1943. The Americans had triumphed at Guadalcanal and the South Pacific was in Allied hands, or perhaps American ones. The Americans benefitted from Australia's policy of keeping its conscript army at home, leaving the smaller volunteer army to fight its way towards Japan, island by island in the wake of the US marines. This fighting was some of the most severe of the war, due to MacArthur's strategy of side-stepping strongly-held positions, leaving them to be 'mopped up' by the Australians.

Australian prisoners of the Japanese, 23,000 of them, were treated, on the Burma-Siam railway and at camps like Changi, with something less than compassion. Australian nurses were no safer than the troops: 22 who surrendered after the fall of Singapore were lined up on a beach at Banka Island and machine-gunned, and all but one died.

One thousand Japanese prisoners-of-war held in the New South Wales prison camp of Cowra broke out to redeem their dishonour and commit suicide. Many succeeded, some under trains, some by disembowelling themselves, or by hanging or burning. It was a bizarre incident which was kept quiet by the authorities.

### ANZAAC Pact
Australia felt it had come of age in the Pacific and was annoyed when it was excluded from the meeting between Churchill and Roosevelt at Cairo in November 1943. The Cairo Conference was to consider the whole course of the war against Japan and the best and quickest way of ensuring her surrender.

In reply to this snub, Australia and New Zealand signed the ANZAAC Pact, which said that both nations must be consulted when matters concerning the Pacific were discussed. As Robert Lacour-Gayet says, this looked to the Americans, suspiciously like a version of the Monroe Doctrine, which laid down similar principles about their own 'back yard' in Central America and the Caribbean. They were not pleased, but had to put up with it since they were not told until the accord had been signed.

John Curtin's health had long caused concern. He was not a strong man, particularly after a heart attack in 1944, but he refused to reduce his commitment to the war effort and his concern for all aspects of the nation's well-being. It was too great a strain and he died some months before the end of the war. He was succeeded by Ben Chifley who saw through the last weeks of fighting, the surrender of Japan and the dawn of a new day.

# 7.
# LUCKY
# COUNTRY

Industrially, Australia emerged from the Second World War much healthier than she had from the First. She had produced a large percentage of her war needs, and the process of industrialization, which had been hampered by the men, money and markets policy, shot forward. The number of men employed in factories went up by 250,000 between 1939 and 1945, and with peace the demand continued to rise. This was reflected in the Labor policy of greater immigration, from Europe as well as the traditional source of the United Kingdom.

## Immigrants

The slogan was 'Populate or Perish', and the government intended to increase the national population of just over seven million. Coloured people were still not welcome, but refugees (reffos) from the horrors of Europe were encouraged – though the more 'Anglo-Saxon' the better.

In the 20 years between 1949 and 1969 two million 'New Australians' arrived to make a better life. The British were given an assisted passage (or a free one in the case of ex-service personnel). Other Europeans received less help and had to cope with more strangeness. Chris Maroukis came from Greece to Melbourne in the early 1950s:

'When we arrived it was autumn, a very foggy day, and we weren't able to see anything of the city. From the ship we were taken straight away into trains and they shifted us 150 miles from Melbourne to a migrant centre. We had to stay there until they placed us in jobs. Sometimes that was difficult to do and many of the new arrivals escaped from the camp and they were trying to make their own way and find work for themselves . . . and one of them was me! One night I escaped and took a train to Sydney where I learnt you could make good money in north Queensland cutting sugar cane. So with six other young men I went. We stayed there about three months but that was all. I went straight back and got jobs in factories – the same thing that tens of thousands of others were doing.'

At the beginning Maroukis found a certain amount of prejudice: 'It was very obvious that there was prejudice against migrants generally. For a portion of the population we were not very welcome. But though it was a problem it wasn't the main one for Greeks, Italians and others.'

Language and culture differences were, difficult and sometimes impossible to overcome, particularly for the old. But for most, like Maroukis, who settled in Melbourne, married and had children, Australia became home. This wasn't to say that all the old ways were left behind. Theatres, newspapers and restaurants soon burgeoned to serve their individual communities. The richness of European and Asian cuisine began to attract ordinary Australians and encouraged the growth of a multicultural society.

## Parties and policies

Social policy under Labor introduced widow's pensions and health benefits, but Chifley found he had problems with his erstwhile allies, the unions, and with the coal-miners in particular.

The miners had called a strike, demanding a 35-hour week. Chifley did not hesitate before calling in the army to mine the coal. He froze the union's funds and took the leadership to court, where they were fined. The strike was broken – in exemplary conservative style. Chifley's next move was not to prove so popular. Nationalization of the banks had long been a Labor dream which turned sour when the party tried to push it through in the face of a hostile business community. Parliament passed the bill, but it was declared unconstitutional by the High Court. Chifley appealed to the Privy Council in London, but the judgement went against him just as a general election was called. Labor did not fare well.

The old Country Party and a new force, the Liberal Party (in fact and policy conservative) were against them. Robert Menzies had emerged from his political fall of 1941 with new ambition and more vigour than ever. The Liberal Party, he said, would be progressive, willing to experiment, believing in individual enterprise but not reactionary, a party which looked to England with respect but understood the need for Pacific alliances. In short, all things to all men except socialists, with the reassuringly solid figure of Menzies at the helm. The nation wanted those things enough to ensure a Liberal-Country coalition which kept Menzies in power for 16 years.

Petrol rationing was removed and public works programmes started or, in the case of the Snowy Mountains Hydro-Electric scheme, continued. Mineral wealth was discovered and mined in ever-increasing amounts. At Mount Isa in Queensland, uranium, silver, zinc and copper were discovered in 1954, and within years the area became the world's largest producer of these minerals. Mineral deposits were found at hundreds of other sites across the country and pointed to a future of unlimited potential.

## Communism and the Petrov Affair

When the United Nations became involved in the Korean War, Australia joined America and Britain in sending an armed force. This raised the nation's stock in the United States, and Menzies made a visit to Washington where he negotiated a $250 million loan.

On his return, in the spirit of Senator Joseph McCarthy, he tried to ban the Communist Party of Australia. Considering the nation's democratic tradition, there was a surprising amount of support for the move, but in the end it was declared unconstitutional by the courts. Menzies called for a referendum, and lost. The anti-libertarian aspects of the act had caused disquiet and this, combined with a tradition of answering 'no' to referendum questions, resulted in 51 per cent against him.

Labor were unable to capitalize on this reverse. Ben Chifley had died in 1951 and his successors could not provide the policies or leadership to overcome a booming economy and the tax cuts which were linked in the popular mind with Robert Menzies. In traditional style, Labor also engaged in continual squabbling between the left and the Irish-Catholic wings of the party. With no Curtin to calm passions, the question of communist influence in the party and the trade unions became a bitter divide.

Things weren't helped by the Petrov Affair. This concerned the defection of a Russian husband and wife spy team. It was thrilling stuff, with Mrs Petrov snatched back by two Russian secret policemen who looked, it was said, like hoods in a third-rate gangster movie. There was a high-speed car chase and she was rescued from the very steps of the plane which was to whisk her back to Russia.

Menzies set up a Royal Commission to examine the papers the Petrovs handed over to the Australian authorities. These documents revealed that three of Labor leader Evatt's staff were unwitting sources of information to Soviet agents. Evatt refused to believe

the charge and said the documents were forgeries.
They weren't; indeed they showed conclusively that the
Russians had been infiltrating the union movement
much as they had in Europe.

Evatt was discredited and the right wing of the
party, under B.A. Santamaria and the redoubtable
Archbishop Mannix, attacked communists in the
unions through the National Catholic Rural Movement.
The fighting, though bloodless, resulted in a split in
the party. Almost as a by-product, communist influence
in the organizations of the left was curtailed and never
recovered.

**Foreign policy**
In his foreign policy Menzies wasn't always the
'Queen's Man' he presented for domestic consumption.
He was aware of the importance of good relations with
the United States and followed their line in recognizing
Chiang Kai-shek while London accepted the credentials
of the communist government in Beijing. He went on to
sign the ANZUS Pact in 1951, enunciating the
principle that America would come to the aid of
Australia and New Zealand if they were attacked . . .
and if Congress agreed.

The Suez débâcle saw Menzies again on the British
side, visiting President Nasser with messages from
Anthony Eden. He received the Egyptian leader's
rejection with slightly bemused anger, as though the
refusal of British condenscension was beyond his
comprehension. This apart, Australia was no longer
having 'two bob each way on defence', as Humphrey
McQueen says; her commitment was to America. The
establishment of the North-West Cape communication
base in the early 1960s locked her into the US
information and defence network for the foreseeable
future.

The ANZUS Pact reflected a continuing suspicion of
Japan, but in the 1960s Japan began to take a larger
proportion of Australian exports – not only wool and

dairy products, but minerals. Australia was becoming the resource bowl for Asia, a profitable position but not one with an unclouded future.

## Atomic tests

Another issue which would cause concern in the future was the testing of British atom bombs on the Monte Bello Islands in 1952 and, over the next decade, at Maralinga in South Australia, a site sacred to the local Aborigines who were not consulted or warned about the nature of the tests. Yami Lester was 12 at the time of the detonations and remembers:

> 'Soldiers coming in army trucks and talking to the adults and . . . I didn't know what they were talking about, I think it was about the test, and they went away. Then one morning we all heard the loud explosion and, I don't know how many hours later, the black mist came over to our camp and went over us, coming from the south. And that was Totem One, Emu test, 1953. When we heard that explosion we were 170 kilometres north. I was worried about people getting sick. People being scared . . .'

A Commission was set up in the 1980s to establish the facts. It placed most of the responsibility upon Britain and recommended that she clean up the test sites and remove the thousands of radio-active metal fragments scattered across miles of desert. The Commission said Australia should compensate the Aborigines who were moved, as Yami Lester recalls, 'south, away from their homelands, down to somebody's country'. Lester also remembers 'people being sick . . . some people vomiting . . . some getting skin rash and skin trouble and still having that skin trouble now'. These experiences prompted him in later years, despite his blindness which he claims was caused by the tests, to tell the story from the Aborigines' point of view.

Robert Menzies had no qualms about the tests. He said Australia's vast spaces were a prime and safe place where no conceivable injury would occur.

## No longer in the home counties

On the social front, life changed comparatively little during the Menzies year. Television was introduced; popular culture, from portable record-players to gambling machines, flourished but the accent was still British. The novelist and poet David Malouf recalls his schooldays:

'It takes people a long time to get over the "idea" and see what the reality is. I grew up in Brisbane – it was a very old-fashioned place and we simply lived as if we were living in the home counties. We dressed at every time of the year with jackets, and ties and long trousers. When I went to school, to a good public school, we sat, in the month of February [high summer] wearing flannel suits and ties and we weren't allowed to take our jackets off because gentlemen didn't sweat. Each night [we had] huge English style stews, with a proper roast dinner on Sundays, and that was always followed by boiled pudding. That was simply because of this idea that we were English-speaking people and this was the way such people lived. And we never looked around and asked if this life was in any way relevant to the climate and the natural landscape we were living in. But then, at some point, that "idea" began to fail and people looked out the window and saw they weren't living in the home counties of England.'

Indeed they weren't and any number of young writers, artists and film-makers growing up with Malouf were feeling the same impatience. The time would come when they would destroy the idea that Australian culture should bow to everything that came from Britain. Even in the 1960s, homegrown ideas and imports from America were producing a real change in attitude and an increase in confidence. Questions of politics, race and gender were no longer forbidden topics.

**Vietnam**

One of Menzies' last official acts, before his retirement in 1965, was to commit Australian troops to Vietnam. His successors, Holt, Gorton and MacMahon, continued this policy of 'all the way with LBJ'. The country was divided over this support and the sending of conscript soldiers chosen by lottery. On 8th May 1970, 70,000 people gathered in Melbourne for a day of national protest. The president of the ACTU (the Trades Union Council), the popular and powerful Bob Hawke, called the gathering the most significant example of public participation in a public event.

At the height of the fighting in Vietnam, Australia contributed 6,300 men, more than half of them regular soldiers, but in the early 1970s her attitude began to change. After 23 years out of office, a Labor government under a vital new leader would soon achieve success. The radical turn of the nation, the opposition to involvement in Vietnam, would be reflected in parliament.

GOUGH WHITLAM

'I was very enthusiastic about Gough Whitlam, because it seemed to me that he had captured the essence of what Labor stood for in Australia. He was one of those gifted men who believed that the Labor movement could create a society in which there was equal opportunity for all people – the descendants of the British, the Irish, the Asians, without any infringements on liberty, without spiritual poverty, without conformism and without pandering to mediocrity. I think he believed

passionately that the circumstances were right for
the creation of an indigenous culture in Australia.'

Manning Clark, like millions of his fellow
Australians, welcomed the Whitlam government of
1972 as a wind of change that would alter the course of
the country.

During their first days in office, Labor created 10
new ministries and made it clear that they would
waste no time sweeping away the legacy of 23 years of
complacency. Communist China was recognized; troops
were recalled from Vietnam; support for Rhodesia's
UDI was withdrawn; tax was removed from
contraceptives; massive funds were given to the
Aborigines; there were reforms in health care and
benefits; national parks were created; educational
advances were made and the Australian Council was
founded. It wasn't so much a wind as a hurricane
which blew from Canberra.

This centralism, a keystone of Whitlam's policy, did
not meet with general approval. States like
Queensland and Western Australia, who had little to
say for federalism at the best of times, began turning
dark glances on the capital. There was nothing they
could do to begin with, the rush of new legislation was
just too great, but conservatives everywhere decided 'to
endure for a while and live for a happier day'.

The rest of society relaxed. MacDonald's hamburgers
opened their first takeaway, though Colonel Sanders
had been selling chicken since 1968. Plastic wine boxes
appeared and soon became as Australian as kangaroos.
Homosexuality among adults was legalized, although
more than 10 years later bars in Queensland were
forbidden to serve 'deviants'. Eating became more
entertaining with the spread of immigrant and
homegrown cookery. Credit cards were introduced and
used increasingly. When Sydney Opera House was
opened, an Aboriginal actor balanced on one of the
sails and declaimed a poem. A women's adviser was

appointed and Australian feminism thrived, except among the surfing community.

Federal funding for writers was increased to one million dollars. There were plans to cut all ties with Britain and to replace state governments with regional councils. It was a boom time, financed by the wealth of the country's minerals. With handfuls of Australia, the country was buying the benefits of American and Japanese high-tech. It was all working; the atmosphere was heady indeed. In 1974 the Australian dollar was worth 1·44 US dollars. The country could, it seemed, do whatever it wanted.

## New Guinea

One of Whitlam's first concerns was the status of New Guinea. Under Australian control since the First World War, New Guinea had missed out in the worldwide move against colonialism. Australia had introduced only the most elementary schooling system, and had treated its subjects with an arrogance and brutality which was a caricature of the excesses of imperialism.

The postwar Labor government had promised independence, as had subsequent administrations, but the dates had always been decades away 'when the Papuans were ready to take over their own affairs'. How they were to achieve that under a system which discouraged education beyond a basic level was not explained. In the early 1960s a National Assembly was introduced but was ineffectual due to its members' inexperience. It was not until the formation of Pangu Pati, a home-grown political union under Michael Samore, that the native voice began to be heard. By 1972 Pangu formed a coalition with enough independent members, reflecting the tribal nature of the society, to become a government which voted for full internal self-determination. This wish was honoured by the Whitlam government.

## Cyclone Tracy

Nature, so important in Australian life, exhibited her power during 1974, when Darwin was struck and virtually demolished by cyclone Tracy.

The winds hit on Christmas Day. The city was unprepared. The Northern Territories were not then self-governing, and local and federal emergency services did not cohere. Houses were ripped apart, cars thrown through the air, ships sank in the harbour and, due to more errors, warnings about the eye of the storm were missed. Many survivors crawled from shelter thinking the storm was over, only to experience another three hours of horror in the open.

Young children were torn from the grasp of their parents; 90 per cent of buildings in the city were destroyed; 65 people died; 150 were injured.

The storm lasted for seven hours and, as with the wartime bombing, prompted a mass evacuation. The federal government moved fast. Relief was organized and pledges made for the rebuilding of the city in more suitable materials. One thing no one could promise was that it would never happen again. Everyone knows that it will.


## Whitlam's errors

Whitlam's support was nationwide but spread thin. His brand of centralized socialism appealed to what has been called the BA DipEd class, a vocal and active minority, but a minority nonetheless.

Many felt that extra spending on social policies and on the arts – over a million dollars was paid by the National Gallery for an abstract painting, 'Blue Poles' – reflected an abstract approach to government in general. Gough was on the bridge, but who was steering the ship? Australia was beginning to feel the pressure of an economic decline which didn't help Whitlam's image. Neither did a series of government scandals. There were suspicions that Whitlam chose his ministers poorly, and was sometimes led into unwise policies.

The loans blunder was one such. The idea was perhaps sound and the intention good: to buy Australia back from foreign investors, not with money borrowed from the West but with a massive loan from the Arab oil countries. Negotiations were set up secretly with shady dealers, and in the end it all fell apart. The scandal was tailor-made for the media who had executed a quick turnabout and were now attacking the government. The decline accelerated. Unemployment crept up to six per cent. It began to seem that the mineral boom was past its peak and that only a small proportion of the profits had ever reached Australian hands.

### 'Nothing will save the Governor General'

Malcom Fraser, the new Liberal leader, was pressing for an election when events took an unexpected course. The government had a majority in the House of Representatives, but could not get its Supply (or Finance) Bill through the Senate.

The passage of the bill should have been easy but a Labor senator from Queensland had died. Rather than replace him with a member of the same party as custom dictated, the autocratic Queensland Premier, Joh Bjelke-Petersen, who had no love for Whitlam, put up an Independent. This allowed the Liberals to block the bill and threaten the Labor Government with bankruptcy. Whitlam felt that if he held his ground and refused to withdraw the bill, the opposition would crack. A ruling government had never gone bankrupt and if it were to do so now Australia's image would be muddied.

It didn't come to that. On 11th November 1975, Sir John Kerr, the Governor-General, the Queen's representative, sacked Whitlam. His proclamation ended with the words, 'God save the Queen'. Whitlam responded, 'Well may we say "God save the Queen",

because nothing will save the Governor-General.'
Malcolm Fraser was branded Kerr's cur. There were
calls for a general strike, mass demonstrations, a move
for a declaration of independence . . . but in the election
which followed Fraser and his Liberal Party were
victorious. The media were able to create in the minds
of the Australian electorate the idea that the
Australian dream was in danger. 'Look out! Your right
to own property, your right to your block of land, your
garden, is in jeopardy. Play safe. Turn to the
conservatives.'

Just as it had after the First World War and the
Second, the nation took the safe option, and not only
through the ballot box. Industry, the media, the Civil
Service – the places where real power lay – also turned
against Whitlam and cut down a man who possessed a
vision of the future rather than a programme of
legislation: a vision which, in the arts, in social policy,
in the participation of ordinary people in government,
persisted after his fall and was crystallized, rather
than destroyed, by the action of Sir John Kerr *in loco
Britannia*.

### Liberal government

Under Malcolm Fraser's Liberal government the nation
stabilized as much as the oil crisis would allow. For the
first time the country population increased faster than
that of the cities. The boat people began to arrive from
Vietnam and were generally welcomed. Gourmets
stopped eating Australian oysters. Robert Menzies died
in 1978. The ecology movement began to have an effect
on national policy through public calls to save the
cities' green areas from developers.

Aborigines, feeling new powers after the Whitlam
years, continued to agitate for land rights in the face of
a mining industry desperate to expand. In Queensland
in 1977, Aboriginal Senator Neville Bonner was
refused service in a bar: 'We don't serve darkies here'.
In the rest of the state Aborigines had no officially-

recognized land, though reserves (one per cent of the land) are meant to be administered by elected Aboriginal councils. These can be overruled by the white managers on the spot or by officials in Brisbane and, in effect, have no real power at all. Western Australia maintains the state has no discrimination. If Aborigines want land, they can buy it at the going rate. If they can get a job and if the job they get pays anything over subsistence.

In the Northern Territories, which achieved self-government in 1978, the situation is complicated by the new legislators trying to come to terms with agreements previously made between local tribes and the federal government in Canberra. It is claimed that mining and cattle farming were made impossible by some of these arrangements. The situation remains fraught and complex, though the Pitjantjantara people have regained their ancient rights and responsibilities to Uluru, the monolith of Ayers Rock. In Tasmania Aboriginal descendants are still waiting for recognition of their ownership of the island; in Victoria claims are being considered; South Australia has returned much, again to the Pitjantjantara people, and is negotiating over the Maralinga test site. New South Wales is also full of good intentions, though none of these last four states has the tension engendered by mining in the more 'frontier' regions. Even so, disputes do occur. In the town of Moree, during the high summer of 1982, a pub fight exploded into a mini race riot in which a young Aborigine was shot dead.

## Labor returns

Malcolm Fraser went to the country in March 1983, confident he could beat a still disorganized Labor Party, but Labor, for once, devoted its energies to victory. The party deposed its leader, Hayden, in favour of a man who had been in parliament just two years, but had, as leader of the ACTU, been a national figure for a long time. Unlike the intellectual Whitlam,

Bob Hawke looked, sounded, drank, philandered and wept like everybody's idea of an ordinary Aussie. A brash exterior hid a brilliant mind, a degree of intellectual arrogance and the certainty that he was at least as well qualified to lead the nation as the traditional power brokers. His first years were eased by the ending of a long drought and a small economic upturn. It did not last, though Hawke was able to persuade the nation that economies must be made, and in July 1987 he was returned for a third term as Prime Minister.

### 'Lucky country'

Donald Horne first used the phrase, now a cultural cliché, 'the lucky country', meaning that, given the ineptitude of its managers, the nation was lucky to have survived as long and comfortably as it had.

That was in the late 1960s. By the middle 1980s the luck was running out and reality was beginning to show through. The nation had been living off high bulk exports of minerals, in many cases owned by America and Japan. For years Australian politicians and labour leaders had been almost racist in their warnings and fears of Japan, but all the time they had been giving large parts of the nation's wealth into the hands of the 'enemy'. In return they were buying, rather than making, sophisticated manufactured goods. Export confidence fell and, when the mineral market flattened out, the profits that had fuelled Australia's future vanished.

It was, in a way, the old story of the New South Wales Corps looking abroad for their profit, bringing in imports of rum, rather than creating industries at Sydney Cove. Australian businessmen and politicians will have to find a new confidence and a new direction. And if nothing else, the European experience has shown that in Australia almost anything is possible for those with the vision and energy to achieve it . . . and the courage to pay the price and live with it.

It is possible that the whites will no longer hold Australia in the distant future or that, if they do,m they will no longer be white. Aborigine and European may come together to live with the land or tear it apart in their struggles. There may be one country or many . . . there may be, as Rex Ingamells says in his poem, *History*:

> 'Deserted station-houses, quiet in drought.
> Bones of cattle, camels, horses, men.'

or perhaps:

> 'Cities growing up,
> towering into the future;
> and this land's destined
> vast cities of imagination.'

BORDERS
REGIONAL
LIBRARY

# CHRONOLOGY

40,000 BC   Aborigines started arriving.

1606        Torres sails between New Guinea and Australia.

1636        Anthony van Diemen arrives in Dutch East Indies for explorations.

1642        Tasman's first voyage. The discovery of Tasmania.

1644        Tasman's second voyage during which he maps the Tasmanian north coast.

1699        Dampier lands in the west of Tasmania. Aborigines in touch with Indonesian fishermen in the north.

1770        Captain Cook lands at Botany Bay, sails up the east coast of Australia and takes possession of New South Wales.

1788        First fleet arrives under Arthur Phillip. Sydney founded.

1790        Second fleet arrives.

1795        Captain John Hunter becomes Governor.

1798        Bass and Flinders established that Tasmania is an island.

1799        Philip King becomes Governor.

1801        Flinders circumnavigates the continent.

1803        Death of Pemulway. Tasmania settled under Collins.

1804        Revolt of Irish convicts put down.

1806        Bligh arrives as Governor.

| | |
|---|---|
| 1808 | Rum rebellion. Bligh overthrown by MacArthur. |
| 1809 | Macquarie arrives. |
| 1813 | Crossing of the Blue Mountains by Blaxland, Lawson and Wentworth. |
| 1821 | Sir Thomas Brisbane appointed Governor. |
| 1825 | Tasmania separated from New South Wales. |
| 1827 | Hume and Hovel reach site of Melbourne. |
| 1828 | Sturt's first journey, discovers River Darling. |
| 1829 | Sturt's second journey. Western Australia founded. |
| 1834 | Founding of South Australia. |
| 1838 | Myall Creek massacre. |
| 1840 | Transportation to New South Wales ends. |
| 1841 | Eyre and Wylie cross Nullarbor plain. |
| 1842 | Representative government in New South Wales. |
| 1848 | Leichhardt vanishes while trying to cross the continent. |
| 1849 | Convicts are transported to Western Australia. |
| 1851 | Gold rush in New South Wales and Victoria. |
| 1853 | Transportation to Tasmania stops. |
| 1854 | Eureka stockade. |
| 1855 | New South Wales, Tasmania, South Australia and Victoria achieve parliamentary government. |
| 1859 | Queensland founded. |
| 1860 | Death of Burke, Wills and Gray trying to cross Australia from south to north. Riots against Chinese at Lambing Flats. |
| 1862 | McDuall Stuart crossed continent. |
| 1867 | Duke of Edinburgh's visit. |
| 1872 | Intercontinental cable link |
| 1883 | Death of Ned Kelly. Queensland occupies New Guinea. |
| 1891 | Labor party emerges. |
| 1893 | Gold discovered in Western Australia. |

| | |
|---|---|
| 1899 | Australian troops in Boer War. |
| 1901 | Federation. |
| 1907 | Fair wage established. |
| 1915 | Gallipoli. William Hughes becomes Prime Minister. |
| 1916 | Conscription row. Hughes leads national government. |
| 1922 | 'Men, money and markets' policy under Bruce. |
| 1939 | Robert Menzies becomes Prime Minister. Second World War. |
| 1941 | Menzies forced out; Curtin becomes Prime Minister. Pearl Habor. |
| 1942 | Singapore falls to Japanese. Darwin bombed. American troops in Australia. |
| 1943 | Victory in New Guinea. |
| 1944 | ANZAAC Pact. |
| 1949 | Menzies returns to power at the head of Liberal Party. |
| 1951 | Australian troops in Korea. ANZUS Pact. Menzies tries to ban Communist party. |
| 1952 | Testing of atom bombs begins. |
| 1954 | Petrov Affair. |
| 1956 | Labor split. Melbourne Olympics. |
| 1965 | Aboriginal freedom rides. Australian troops in Vietnam. |
| 1966 | Menzies resigns. |
| 1972 | Labor Party returns to power after 23 years. Aborigines set up 'tent embassy' on the lawns of Government House. |
| 1975 | Sir John Kerr sacks Gough Whitlam. |
| 1978 | Northern Territories achieve self government. |
| 1982 | Racial trouble flares in Moree. |
| 1983 | Bob Hawke elected Prime Minister. |
| 1985 | Commission on atom tests delivers report. |
| 1988 | Bicentenary of first white settlement. |

# FURTHER READING

R M and C H Berndt, *The First Australians*, Ure Smith, 1952

Geoffrey Blainey, *The Tyranny of Distance*, Macmillan, 1975; *Triumph of the Nomads*, Macmillan, 1976

Max Brown, *Ned Kelly: Australian Son*, Angus and Robertson, 1941

Don Charlwood, *The Long Farewell*, Penguin Books, 1983

Linda Christmas, *The Ribbon and the Ragged Square*, Viking, 1986

Manning Clarke, *Select Documents in Australian History Vols 1 and 2*, Angus and Robertson, 1950; *A Short History of Australia*, Macmillan, 1982

M Bernard Eldershaw, *Phillip of Australia*, Angus and Robertson, 1972

M H Ellis, *Lachlan Macquarie*, Angus and Robertson, 1947

Bill Gammage, *The Broken Years: Australian Soldiers in the Great War*, Australian National University Press, 1974

Kevin Gilbert, *Living Black*, Penguin Books, 1978

Harry Gordon, *An Eyewitness History of Australia*, Curry O'Niel, 1976

Harry Heseltine, *The Penguin Book of Australian Verse*, Penguin Books, 1972

Donald Horne, *The Lucky Country*, Penguin Books, 1964; *The Australian People*, Angus and Robertson, 1972

Jennifer Isaacs (ed.), *Australian Dreaming*, Landsowne Press, 1980

Thomas Keneally, *Outback*, Hodder and Stoughton, 1983

Jonathan King and John King, *Philip Gidley King*, Methuen, 1981

Robert Lacour-Gayet, *A Concise History of Australia*, Penguin Books, 1976

John Laffin, *Anzacs at War*, Abelard Schuman, 1965

Henry Lawson, *When the Billy Boils*, Angus and Robertson

Humphrey McQueen, *Social Sketches of Australia 1888–1975*, Penguin Books, 1978

Robert Milliken, *No Conceivable Injury*, Penguin Books, 1986

Alan Moorhead, *Cooper's Creek*, Hamish Hamilton, 1965

Bill Murray, *Crisis, Conflict and Consensus*, Rigby, 1984

Henry Reynolds, *The Other Side of the Frontier: Aboriginal Resistance to the European Invasion of Australia*, Penguin Books, 1982

Jan Roberts, *Massacres to Mining*, Dove, 1978

C D Rowley, *The Destruction of Aboriginal Society*, Penguin Books, 1972

George Rude, *Protest and Punishment*, Oxford University Press, 1978

Watkin Tench, *Sydney's First Four Years* (reprint), Library of Australian History, 1979

John White, *Journal of a Voyage to New South Wales* (reprint), Angus and Robertson, 1962

## ABOUT THE AUTHOR

MIKE WALKER has been a freelance writer for the past eight years and is now well established as an author of drama and radio and television documentaries.

His most recent work has included documentaries on the American Indians, various aspects of social life in Tahiti, Brazil and Bali and, of course, writing the BBC radio series *Australia*, on which this book is based.

Mike Walker is married and lives in Reading.